"In a time when Broadway is g
with its history of erasure, this   _ *in Mind* asks,
how far have we truly come? . . . *Trouble in Mind* is holding up
a mirror to society, especially the sector that considers itself
progressive. Sixty-six years ago, society chose to look away.
Perhaps the play's premiere on Broadway is a sign we are finally
ready to truly look at ourselves."

—DIEP TRAN, NEW YORK THEATRE GUIDE

"A sword-sharp satire . . . Glorious to behold."

—TERRY TEACHOUT, WALL STREET JOURNAL

"Without question, *Trouble in Mind* is an old-fashioned play—
if we understand the term to mean well-built, lean, and clear
of purpose. You absolutely must see it if you care about Black
work on Broadway, American theater, and the evolving state of
our 'canon.'"

—DAVID COTE, OBSERVER

"If a Broadway season in which Black playwrights are substan-
tially represented has been a long time coming, the presence
of one work is especially overdue. *Trouble in Mind* clearly and
potently reflects its era, its enduring freshness speaks to how
much progress has yet to be made."

—ELYSA GARDNER, NEW YORK STAGE REVIEW

"Alice Childress's searing play *Trouble in Mind* has finally made
it to Broadway and the only frustrating thing about the show
is that it has taken this long . . . A play written at the time
of Emmett Till's murder needed to be seen by a crowd who
lived through the murder of George Floyd . . . It will take your
breath away."

—MARK KENNEDY, ASSOCIATED PRESS

"Trenchant . . . To a startling degree, the play anticipates many of the conversations that have taken place in the past two years about the devaluation of Black artists in the theater world."

—ADAM FELDMAN, *TIME OUT NEW YORK*

"*Trouble in Mind* is an intellectually curious play, whose considerations of Black representation in art and liberal smugness make it hauntingly timely. Its layers of biting humor and damning observations hit notes about race, art, and integrity that are no less important for feeling familiar in 2021—especially when you consider that Childress penned this work in the '50s."

—LOVIA GYARKYE, *HOLLYWOOD REPORTER*

"Childress's themes do not feel nearly as distant as they should . . . *Trouble in Mind* was staged Off-Broadway in 1955, just as America was tipping into the civil rights movement, and Childress captured the very live anger of her era, as it was being experienced."

—ARIFA AKBAR, *GUARDIAN*

"Sixty-four years late and right on time, Alice Childress's wise and stirring backstage comedy-drama *Trouble in Mind* is making its long-in-coming Broadway debut. *Trouble in Mind* takes a behind-the-curtain look at the racism, coded prejudice, self-flattery, sexism, and built-in bigotry that Broadway has always professed to eschew . . . To describe the play as prescient would be an understatement. Uncanny rings truer."

—GREG EVANS, *DEADLINE*

"*Trouble in Mind* is an engaging and stirring piece of activist theater which wrestles with the structural problems and racial inequalities at the heart of show business."

—LIZZIE AKITA, *LONDON THEATRE*

"Childress's play still has a lion's bite six decades on and is a rock-solid, ferociously funny, tense piece of writing . . . Her play is a lesson in construction, in the hot-blooded interplay of satire and seriousness. *Trouble in Mind* is just plain good."

—JOHNNY OLEKSINSKI, *NEW YORK POST*

"Written in 1955, the year the Montgomery bus boycott began, Alice Childress's *Trouble in Mind* is about a gifted and passionate Black actress held back by a predominantly white theater world. The fact that Childress's play—funny, startling, and incredibly modern-feeling—isn't in the canon and didn't get a production on Broadway until this year shows how close it comes to the bone."

—JESSIE THOMPSON, *EVENING STANDARD*

"*Trouble in Mind* is not just a theatrical soapbox or a resurrected fusty old work. It is a well-structured play, a backstage comedy-drama filled with portrayals and dialogue that are often quite funny and satirical on the one hand, yet moving and assertive when the time is right."

—HOWARD MILLER, *TALKIN' BROADWAY*

"Some will call Alice Childress prescient, but what is prescience when the events depicted have been occurring for centuries? That's what makes this dynamite play even sadder—after sixty-some years, *Trouble in Mind* couldn't be timelier if it were written yesterday, and the events are as explosive and subversive now as they were in the 1950s."

—DAVID GORDON, *THEATERMANIA*

TROUBLE IN MIND

FORTHCOMING FROM TCG BOOKS ILLUMINATIONS:

Happy Ending and *Day of Absence*
By Douglas Turner Ward

Insurrection: Holding History
By Robert O'Hara

TROUBLE IN MIND

Alice Childress

 ILLUMINATIONS
THEATRE COMMUNICATIONS GROUP / NEW YORK / 2022

Trouble in Mind is published by Theatre Communications Group, Inc., 520 Eighth Avenue, 24th Floor, New York, NY 10018-4156

The publication of *Trouble in Mind* by Alice Childress, through TCG Books Illuminations, is made possible with support by Mellon Foundation.

TCG books are exclusively distributed to the book trade by Consortium Book Sales and Distribution.

Library of Congress Control Numbers
2021045230 (print) / 2021045231 (ebook)
ISBN 978-1-63670-015-1 (paperback) / ISBN 978-1-63670-016-8 (ebook)
A catalog record for this book is available from the Library of Congress.

Cover, book design and composition by Lisa Govan
Cover painting by Alice Neel. Alice Childress, 1950; Oil on canvas; 30 1/8 x 20 1/8 inches; 76.5 x 51.1 cm; Collection of Art Berliner; © The Estate of Alice Neel; Courtesy The Estate of Alice Neel and David Zwirner

First Edition, May 2022

CONTENTS

TROUBLE IN MIND

A Comedy-Drama in Two Acts

PRODUCTION HISTORY

Trouble in Mind opened on Broadway at the American Airlines Theatre on November 18, 2021. It was produced by Roundabout Theatre Company (Todd Haimes, Artistic Director/ CEO; Julia C. Levy, Executive Director; Sydney Beers, Executive Producer; Steve Dow, Chief Administrative Officer). It was directed by Charles Randolph-Wright. The scenic design was by Arnulfo Maldonado, the costume design was by Emilio Sosa, the lighting design was by Kathy A. Perkins, the sound design was by Dan Moses Schreier, hair and wigs were by Cookie Jordan, makeup was by Kirk Cambridge-Del Pesche, and the original music was by Nona Hendryx. The stage manager was Alfredo Macias. The cast was:

WILETTA MAYER	LaChanze
HENRY	Simon Jones
JOHN NEVINS	Brandon Micheal Hall
MILLIE DAVIS	Jessica Frances Dukes
JUDY SEARS	Danielle Campbell
SHELDON FORRESTER	Chuck Cooper
AL MANNERS	Michael Zegen
EDDIE FENTON	Alex Mickiewicz
BILL O'WRAY	Don Stephenson

Trouble in Mind opened at the Greenwich Mews Theatre (Lily Turner, Artistic Director; Stella Holt, Administrative Coordinator) on November 4, 1955, in New York City, and ran for ninety-one performances. The play was directed by Clarice Taylor and Alice Childress. The scenic and lighting design were by Vincent Sorrentino. The stage manager was Howard Augusta. The cast was:

WILETTA MAYER	Clarice Taylor
POP [HENRY]	Liam Lenihan
JOHN NEVILLE [NEVINS]	Charles Bettis
MILLIE DAVIS	Hilda Haynes
JUDITH SEARS	Stephanie Elliot
SHELDON FORRESTER	Howard Augusta
AL MANNERS	James McMahon
EDDIE FENTON	Hal England
HOODAN [BILL O'WRAY]	Johnny Barracuda
SINGER	Louise Kemp

CHARACTERS

WILETTA MAYER

HENRY

JOHN NEVINS

MILLIE DAVIS

JUDY SEARS

SHELDON FORRESTER

AL MANNERS

EDDIE FENTON

BILL O'WRAY

PLACE

A Broadway theater in New York City, 1957.

Act 1

*A Broadway theater in New York City. Ten o'clock Monday morning.
Fall 1957. Blues music in, out after lights up.*

*The stage of the theater. Stage left leads to the outside entrance.
Stage right to upstairs dressing rooms.*

*There are many props and leftovers from the last show: a plaster
fountain with a cupid perched atop, garden furniture, tables, benches,
a trellis, two white armchairs trimmed with gold gilt.*

*Before the curtain rises we hear banging sounds from offstage left,
the banging grows louder and louder.*

*Curtain rises. Wiletta Mayer, a middle-aged actress, appears. She
is attractive and expansive in personality. She carries a purse and a
script. At the moment, she is in quite a huff.*

WILETTA: My Lord, I like to have wore my arm off bangin' on
that door! What you got it locked for?

(Lights up brighter.)

Had me standin' out there in the cold, catchin' my death of
pneumonia!

(Henry, the elderly doorman, enters.)

HENRY: I didn't hear a thing . . . I didn't know . . .

(Wiletta is suddenly moved by the sight of the theater. She holds up her hand for silence, looks out and up at the balcony. She loves the theater. She turns back to Henry.)

WILETTA: A theater always makes me feel that way . . . gotta get still for a second.

HENRY *(Welcomes an old memory)*: You . . . you are Wiletta Mayer . . . more than twenty years ago, in the old Galy Theater . . . *(Wiletta is pleased to be remembered)* You was singin' a number, with the lights changin' color all around you . . . What was the name of that show?

WILETTA: *Brownskin Melody.*

HENRY: That's it . . . and the lights . . .

WILETTA: Was a doggone rainbow.

HENRY: And you looked so pretty and sounded so fine, there's no denyin' it.

WILETTA: Thank you, but I . . . I . . .

(Wiletta hates to admit she doesn't remember him.)

HENRY: I'm Henry.

WILETTA: Mmmmm, you don't say.

HENRY: I was the electrician. Rigged up all those lights and never missed a cue. I'm the doorman here now. I've been in show business over fifty years. I'm the doorman . . . Henry.

WILETTA: That's a nice name. I . . . I sure remember those lights.

HENRY: Bet you can't guess how old I am, I'll betcha.

WILETTA *(Would rather not guess)*: Well . . . you're sure lookin' good.

HENRY: Go ahead, take a guess.

WILETTA *(Being very kind)*: Ohhhhh, I'd say you're in your . . . late fifties.

HENRY *(Laughs proudly)*: I fool 'em all! I'm seventy-eight years old! How's that?

WILETTA: Ohhhh, don't be tellin' it.

(She places her script and purse on the table, removes her coat. Henry takes coat and hangs it on a rack.)

HENRY: You singin' in this new show?

WILETTA: No, I'm actin'. I play the mother.

HENRY *(Hard of hearing)*: How's that?

WILETTA: I'm the mother!

HENRY: Could I run next door and get you some coffee? I'm goin' anyway, no bother.

WILETTA: No, thank you just the same.

HENRY: If you open here, don't let 'em give you dressin' room "C." It's small and it's got no "john" in it . . . excuse me, I mean . . . no commode . . . Miss Mayer.

WILETTA *(Feeling like the star he's made her)*: Thank you, I'll watch out for that.

(Henry reaches for a small chair, changes his mind and draws the gilt armchair to the table.)

HENRY: Make yourself comfortable. The old Galy. Yessir, I'm seventy-eight years old.

WILETTA: Well, I'm not gonna tell you my age. A woman that'll tell her age will tell anything.

HENRY *(Laughs)*: Oh, that's a good one! I'll remember that! A woman that'll tell her age . . . what else?

WILETTA: Will tell anything.

HENRY: *Will* tell. Well, I'll see you a little later.

(He exits stage left.)

WILETTA *(Saying goodbye to the kind of gentle treatment she seldom receives)*: So long.

(She rises and walks downstage, strikes a pose from the "old Galy," and sings a snatch of an old song.)

> Oh, honey babe
> Oh, honey babe . . .

(She pushes the memory aside.)

Yes, indeed!

(John Nevins, a young Negro actor, enters. He tries to look self-assured, but it's obvious that he is new to the theater and fighting hard to control his enthusiasm.)

Good morning. Another early bird! I'm glad they hired you, you read so nice er . . . ah . . .

JOHN: John, John Nevins.

WILETTA: This is new for you, ain't it?

JOHN: Yes, ma'am.

WILETTA: Yes, ma'am? I know you're not a New Yorker, where's your home?

JOHN: Newport News, that's in Virginia.

WILETTA: HOT DOG. I shoulda known anyone as handsome and mannerly as you had to come from my home. Newport News! Think of that! Last name?

JOHN: Nevins, John Nevins.

WILETTA: Wait a minute . . . do you know Estelle Nevins, used to live out on Prairie Road . . . fine-built woman?

JOHN: Guess I do, that's my mother.

WILETTA *(Very touched)*: No, she ain't!

JOHN *(Afraid of oncoming sentiment)*: Yes . . . ah . . . yes she is.

WILETTA: What a day! I went to school with Estelle! She married a fella named Clarence! Used to play baseball. Last time I hit home she had a little baby in the carriage. How many children she got?

JOHN: I'm the only one.

WILETTA: You can't be that little baby in the carriage! Stand up, let me look at you! Brings all of yesterday back to my mind! Tell me, John, is the drugstore still on the corner? Used to be run by a tall, strappin' fella . . . got wavy, black hair . . . and, well, he's kind of devilish . . . Eddie Bentley!

JOHN: Oh yes, Mr. Bentley is still there . . .

WILETTA: Fresh and sassy and . . .

JOHN: But he's gray-haired and very stern and businesslike.

WILETTA *(Very conscious of her age)*: You don't say. Why you want to act? Why don't you make somethin' outta yourself?

JOHN *(Is amazed at this)*: What? Well, I . . .

WILETTA: You look bright enough to be a doctor or even a lawyer maybe . . . You don't have to take what I've been through . . . don't have to take it off 'em.

JOHN: I think the theater is the grandest place in the world, and I plan to go right to the top.

WILETTA *(With good humor)*: Uh-huh, and where do you think I was plannin' to go?

JOHN *(Feeling slightly superior because he thinks he knows more about the craft than Wiletta)*: Ohhh, well . . .

WILETTA *(Quick to sense his feelings)*: Oh, well, what?

JOHN *(Feels a bit chastised)*: Nothing. I know what I want to do. I'm set, decided, and that's that. You're in it, aren't you proud to be a part of it all?

WILETTA: Of what all?

JOHN: Theater.

WILETTA: *Show business*, it's just a business. Colored folks ain't in no theater. You ever do a professional show before?

JOHN: Yes, some Off-Broadway . . . and I've taken classes.

WILETTA: Don't let the man know that. They don't like us to go to school.

JOHN: Oh, now.

WILETTA: They want us to be naturals . . . you know, just born with the gift. 'Course they want you to be experienced too. Tell 'em you was in the last revival of *Porgy and Bess*.

JOHN: I'm a little young for that.

WILETTA: They don't know the difference. You were one of the children.

JOHN: I need this job but . . . must I lie?

WILETTA: Yes. Management hates folks who *need* jobs. They get the least money, the least respect, and most times they don't get the job.

JOHN *(Laughs)*: Got it. I'm always doing great.

WILETTA: But don't get too cocky. They don't like that either. You have to cater to these fools too . . .

JOHN: I'm afraid I don't know how to do that.

WILETTA: Laugh! Laugh at everything they say, makes 'em feel superior.

JOHN: Why do they have to feel superior?

WILETTA: You gonna sit there and pretend you don't know why?

JOHN: I . . . I'd feel silly laughing at everything.

WILETTA: You don't. Sometimes they laugh, you're supposed to look serious, other times they serious, you supposed to laugh.

JOHN *(In polite disagreement)*: Sounds too complicated.

WILETTA *(Warming to her subject)*: Nothin' to it. Suppose the director walks in, looks around, and says . . . *(Mimics Al Manners)* "Well, if the dust around here doesn't choke us to death, we'll be able to freeze in comfort."

JOHN: Yes?

WILETTA: We laugh and dispute him. *(Illustrates)* "Oh, now, Mr. Manners, it ain't that bad!" . . . White folks can't stand unhappy Negroes . . . so laugh, laugh when it ain't funny at all.

JOHN: Sounds kind of Uncle Tommish.

WILETTA: You callin' me a "Tom"?

JOHN: No, ma'am.

WILETTA: Stop sayin' ma'am, it sounds countrified.

JOHN: Yes.

WILETTA: It is Tommish . . . but they do it more than we do. They call it bein' a "yes man." You either do it and stay or don't do it and get out. I can let you in on things that school never heard of . . . 'cause I know what's out here and they don't.

JOHN: Thank you. I guess I'll learn the ropes as I go along.

WILETTA: I'm tellin' you now! Oh, you so lucky! Nobody told me, had to learn it for myself.

(John is trying to hide the fact that he does not relish her instructions.)

Another thing. He's gonna ask your honest opinion about the play. Don't tell him, he don't mean it . . . just say you're crazy about it . . . butter him up.

(This remark really bothers John.)

JOHN: What *do* you think of our play?

WILETTA: Oh, honey, it stinks, ain't nothin' at all. 'Course, if I hear that again, I'll swear you lyin'.

JOHN: Why are you doing it? A flop can't make you but so rich.

WILETTA: Who said it's gonna flop? I said it ain't nothin', but things that aggravate me always *run* for a long time . . . 'cause what bugs me is what sends somebody else, if you know what I mean.

JOHN *(Defensively)*: I studied it thoroughly and . . .

WILETTA: Honey, don't study it, just learn it.

JOHN: I wouldn't, couldn't play anything I didn't believe in . . . I couldn't.

WILETTA (*Understands he's a bit upstage now*): Oh, well, you just a lost ball in the high grass.

(*Millie Davis, a Negro actress about thirty-five years old, enters. She breezes in, beautifully dressed in a mink coat, pastel wool dress and hat, suede shoes and bag.*)

MILLIE: Hi!
WILETTA: Walk, girl! Don't she look good?
MILLIE: Don't look too hard, it's not paid for.

(*Millie models the coat for Wiletta as she talks to John.*)

You got the job! Good for you.

(*Wiletta picks up Millie's newspaper.*)

JOHN: And congratulations to you.

(*Millie takes off her coat and hangs it up.*)

MILLIE: I don't care one way or the other 'cause my husband doesn't want me workin' anyway.
WILETTA: Is he still a dining-car waiter?
MILLIE: I wanted to read for your part but Mr. Manners said I was too young. They always say too young . . . too young.
WILETTA: Hear they're lookin' for a little girl to play Goldilocks, maybe you should try for that.
MILLIE: Oh, funny.
WILETTA (*Commenting on the headlines*): Look at 'em! Throwin' stones at little children, got to call out the militia to go to school.
JOHN: That's terrible.
MILLIE (*Quite proud of her contribution to Little Rock*): A woman pushed me on the subway this mornin' and I was ready for

her! Called her everything but a child of God. She turned purple! Oh, I fixed her!

(Judy Sears, a young actress [white], is heard offstage with Sheldon Forrester, an elderly Negro character man.)

JUDY: This way . . .

SHELDON: Yes, ma'am. Don't hurt yourself.

(Sheldon and Judy enter, Judy first.)

JUDY: Good morning.

(Others respond in unison.)

JOHN: Hello again, glad you made it.

MILLIE: Hi! I'm Millie, that's John, Wiletta, and you're?

JUDY: Judith, just call me Judy.

(Sheldon is bundled in heavy overcoat, two scarves, one outer, one inner.)

SHELDON: And call me Shel!

WILETTA: Sheldon Forrester! So glad to see you! Heard you was sick.

MILLIE: I heard he was dead.

SHELDON: Yes! Some fool wrote a piece in that *Medium Brown Magazine* 'bout me bein' dead. You can see he was lyin'. But I lost a lotta work on accounta that. Doctor says that with plenty of rest and fresh air, I oughta outlive him.

WILETTA: Bet you will, too.

SHELDON: Mr. Manners was lookin' all over for me, said nobody could play this part but me.

MILLIE: Not another soul can do what you're gonna do to it.

SHELDON: Thank you.

(John starts over to Judy but Sheldon stops him.)

Didn't you play in er . . . ah . . . er . . .

WILETTA: He was in the last revival of *Porgy and Bess.* Was one of the children.

(She watches John's reaction to this.)

SHELDON: Yeah, I know I remembered you. He ain't changed much, just bigger. Nice little actor.

JOHN *(Embarrassed)*: Thank you, sir.

WILETTA: Sheldon got a good memory.

MILLIE *(To Judy)*: What're you doing?

SHELDON: She's *Miss* Renard, the Southerner's daughter. Fights her father 'bout the way he's treatin' us.

MILLIE: What I want is a part where I get to fight him.

WILETTA: Ha! That'll be the day!

SHELDON: Bill O'Wray is the father, he's awful nice.

MILLIE: Also wish I'd get to wear some decent clothes sometime. Only chance I get to dress up is offstage. I'll wear them baggy cotton dresses but damn if I'll wear another bandanna.

SHELDON: That's how country people do! But go on the beach today, what do you see? Bandannas. White folks wear 'em! They stylish!

MILLIE: That's a lot of crap!

SHELDON: There you go! You holler when there's no work—when the man give you some, you holler just as loud. Ain't no pleasin' you!

(John starts toward Judy again; this time Millie stops him.)

MILLIE: Last show I was in, I wouldn't even tell my relatives. All I did was shout, "Lord, have mercy!" for almost two hours every night.

WILETTA: Yes, but you did it, so hush! She's played every flower in the garden. Let's see, what was your name in that TV mess?

MILLIE: Never mind.

WILETTA: Gardenia! She was Gardenia! 'Nother thing . . . she was Magnolia, Chrysanthemum was another . . .

MILLIE: And you've done the jewels . . . Crystal, Pearl, Opal!

(Millie laughs.)

JOHN *(Weak, self-conscious laughter)*: Oh, now . . .

(Judy has retreated to one side, trying to hide herself behind a book.)

SHELDON: Do, Lord, let's keep the peace. Last thing I was in, the folks fought and argued so, the man said he'd never do a colored show again . . . and he didn't!

WILETTA: I always say it's the man's play, the man's money, and the man's theater, so what you gonna do? *(To Millie)* You ain't got a pot nor a window. Now, when you get your own . . .

(Sheldon clears his throat to remind them that Judy is listening.)

Honey, er . . . what you say your name was?

JUDY: Judy.

(Wiletta sweeps over to Judy and tries to cover the past argument.)

WILETTA: I know I've seen you in pictures, didn't you make some pictures?

JUDY: No, this is my first job.

JOHN *(Joshing Wiletta)*: Oh, you mustn't tell that because—

WILETTA *(Cutting him off)*: You're just as cute as a new penny.

SHELDON: Sure is.

(A brief moment of silence while they wait for Judy to say something.)

JUDY *(Starts hesitantly but picks up momentum as she goes along)*: Thank you, and er . . . er . . . I hope I can do a good job and that people learn something from this play.

MILLIE: Like what?

JUDY: That people are the same, that people are . . . are . . . well, you know . . . that people are people.

SHELDON: There you go . . . brotherhood of man stuff! Sure!

WILETTA: Yes, indeed. I don't like to think of theater as just a business. Oh, it's the art . . . ain't art a wonderful thing?

MILLIE *(Bald, flat statement to no one in particular)*: People aren't the same.

JUDY: I read twice for the part and there were so many others before me and after me . . . and I was so scared that my voice came out all funny . . . I stumbled on the rug when I went in . . . everything was terrible.

MILLIE *(Another bald, flat statement)*: But you got the job.

JUDY *(Uneasy about Millie's attitude)*: Yes.

JOHN *(To the rescue)*: And all the proud relatives will cheer you on opening night!

JUDY *(Nothing can drown her spirits for long)*: Yes! My mother and father . . . they live in Bridgeport . . . they really don't want me here at all. They keep expecting something *terrible* to happen to me . . . like being murdered or something! But they're awfully sweet and they'll be so happy. *(Abrupt change of subject)* What do you think of the play?

WILETTA: Oh, I never had anything affect me so much in all my life. It's so sad, ain't it sad?

JUDY: Oh, there's some humor.

WILETTA: I'm tellin' you, I almost busted my sides laughin'.

(Sheldon is busy looking in the script.)

JOHN: It has a social theme and something to say.

JUDY: Yes.

WILETTA: Art! Art is a great thing!

MILLIE: It's all right except for a few words here and there . . .
and those Gawd-awful clothes . . .

JOHN: Words, clothes. What about the very meaning?

(Sheldon startles everyone by reading out loud. His finger runs down the page; he skips his cues and reads his lines.)

SHELDON: Mr. Renard, sir, everything is just fine . . . Yes, sir . . .
Thank you, sir . . . Yes, sirreee, I sure will . . . I know . . .
Yes, sir . . . But iffen, iffen . . .

(He pauses to question the word.)

Iffen?

(Now he understands.)

Iffen you don't mind, we'd like to use the barn.

MILLIE: Iffen.

SHELDON: Hush, Millie, so I can get these lines, I'm not a good
reader, you know.

MILLIE: Iffen you forget one, just keep shakin' your head.

(Offstage we hear a door slam. Al Manners, the director [white], is giving Eddie Fenton, the stage manager [white], a friendly chastising.)

MANNERS *(Offstage)*: Eddie, why? Why do you do it?

EDDIE *(Offstage)*: I didn't know.

SHELDON *(Assumes a very studious air and begins to study his script earnestly)*: Mr. Manners.

(Eddie and Manners enter, followed by Henry. Eddie is eager and quick. He carries a portfolio and a stack of scripts. Manners is in his early forties, hatless, a well-tweeded product of Hollywood. He is a bundle of energy, considerate and understanding after his own fashion; selfish and tactless after ours. Henry is following him around, ready to write out a coffee order.)

EDDIE *(With a smile)*: You asked my opinion.

MANNERS: That, my friend, was a mistake.

EDDIE *(Laughing while cast smiles in anticipation of Manners's words)*: Okay, I admit you were right, you were.

MANNERS *(Enjoying himself)*: Of course I was. *(To company)* All of his taste is in his mouth!

(Burst of company laughter, especially from Sheldon and Wiletta.)

EDDIE *(Playfully correcting Manners)*: All right, Al, play fair . . . uncle . . . a truce.

MANNERS *(To company)*: Greetings to New York's finest.

ALL: Good morning . . . Flatterer . . . Hello . . . Good morning.

MANNERS *(To Henry)*: Coffee all around the room and count yourself in.

(Manners hands him a bill.)

Rolls? Cake? No . . . how about danish . . . all right?

ALL: Yes . . . Sure . . . Anything . . . Okay.

SHELDON: I like doughnuts, those jelly doughnuts.

MANNERS: Jelly doughnuts! What a horrible thought. Get danish . . . all right?

ALL: Sure . . . Anything . . . That's fine.

MANNERS *(After Henry exits)*: If you were looking for that type, you could never find it! A real character.

JOHN: One of the old forty-niners.

MANNERS: No, no . . . not quite that . . .

(Manners turns off that faucet and quickly switches to another.)

Everyone on speaking terms?

ALL: Of course . . . Old friends . . . Oh, yes . . . Sure.

(Manners opens the portfolio with a flourish.)

MANNERS: Best scenic design you've ever laid eyes on.

(All gasp and sigh as they gather around him. They are quite impressed with the sketch. Judy is very close, and Manners looks down at her hair and neck which is perched right under his nostrils. Judy can feel his breath on her neck. She turns suddenly and Manners backs away a trifle.)

You er . . . wear a beautiful dress in the third act and I wanted to see if you have nice shoulders.

(Judy backs away slightly.)

I wasn't planning to attack you.

(Cast laughs.)

MILLIE: I got nice shoulders. You got one of those dresses for me?

SHELDON *(Determined to enjoy everything)*: Ha! He wasn't gonna attack her!

MANNERS *(Suddenly changes faucets again)*: Oh, I'm so weary.

EDDIE *(Running interference)*: He was with Melton on this sketch until four A.M.

MANNERS: Four thirty.

EDDIE: Four thirty.

MANNERS *(Swoops down on Wiletta)*: Ahhhhh, this is my sweetheart!

WILETTA *(With mock severity)*: Go on! Go 'way! Ain't speakin' to you! He won't eat, he won't sleep, he's just terrible! I'm mad with you.

SHELDON: Gonna ruin your health like that!

WILETTA: Gonna kill himself!

MANNERS: Bawl me out, I deserve it.

EDDIE: Melton is so stubborn, won't change a line.

MANNERS: But he did.

EDDIE: Yes, but so stubborn.

MANNERS: A genius should be stubborn. *(Pointing index finger at Sheldon)* Right?

SHELDON *(Snaps his fingers and points back)*: There you go!

(Cast laughs.)

MANNERS *(To Wiletta)*: You'd better speak to me. This is my girl, we did a picture together.

CAST *(Ad-lib)*: Really? How nice. She sure did. That's right.

MANNERS *(As though it's been centuries)*: Ohhhhhh, years and years ago.

MILLIE *(To Wiletta)*: Remember that?

MANNERS: He and I worked together too.

SHELDON *(Proudly)*: I was helpin' the Confederate Army.

MANNERS: And what a chestnut: guns, cannons, drums, Indians, slaves, hearts and flowers, sex and Civil War . . . on wide screen!

JUDY: Oh, just horrible.

MANNERS *(Touchy about outside criticism)*: But it had something, wasn't the worst . . . I twisted myself out of shape to build this guy's part. It was really a sympathetic character.

SHELDON: Sure, everybody was sorry for me.

MANNERS *(To John)*: Hear you went to college. You're so modest you need a press agent.

SHELDON: He was one of the children in the last revival of *Porgy and Bess*.

MANNERS: Ohhhh, yes . . . nice clean job.

JUDY: I'm not modest. I finished the Yale drama course. Girls . . . girls . . . can go to the Yale drama . . .

MANNERS: Yale. I'm impressed.

JUDY: You're teasing.

MANNERS: No, you are. Well, where are we? Bill O'Wray is out until tomorrow, he's in a rehearsal for a TV show tonight.

(Proper sighs of regret from cast.)

WILETTA: Oh, I was lookin' forward to seein' him today.

SHELDON: Yeah, yeah, nice fella.

MANNERS: Works all the time. *(Now some attention for Millie)* You look gorgeous. This gal has such a flair for clothes. How do you do it?

(Millie is pleased. Manners changes the subject.)

Ted Bronson is one of our finest writers.

WILETTA: Knows art, knows it.

EDDIE: He was up for an award.

MANNERS: Really, Eddie. I wish you'd let me tell it.

EDDIE: I'm sorry.

MANNERS: Ted's been out on the coast batting out commercial stuff . . . meat grinder . . . he's in Europe now . . . Italy . . . about a week before he can get back . . . he did this *Chaos in Belleville* a while back. Producers gave him nothing but howls . . . "It's ahead of the times!" "Why stick your neck out?" "Why you?"

SHELDON *(Raises his hand, speaks after Manners gives him a nod)*: Who is chaos?

EDDIE: Oh, no.

JOHN: *Who?*

MANNERS *(Holds up his hand for silence)*: Chaos means er . . . ah, confusion. *Confusion in Belleville*, confusion in a small town.

SHELDON: Ohhhhhh.

MANNERS: I was casually talking to Ted about the er . . . er, race situation, kicking a few things around . . . dynamic subject, hard to come to grips with on the screen, TV, anywhere . . . explosive subject. Suddenly he reaches to the bottom shelf and comes up with *Chaos*. I flipped a few pages . . . when I read it, bells rang. This is *now*, we're living this, who's in the headlines these days?

(Eloquent pause.)

SHELDON: How 'bout that Montgomery, Alabama? Made the bus company lose one, cold, cash, billion dollars!

JOHN: Not a billion.

MANNERS: Here was a contribution to the elimination of . . .

SHELDON: I know what I read!

MANNERS: A story of Negro rights that . . .

SHELDON: How 'bout them buses!

JUDY: And they're absolutely right.

MILLIE: Who's right?

MANNERS: A contribution that really . . .

JUDY: The colored people.

MANNERS: leads to a clearer understanding . . .

MILLIE: Oh, I thought you meant the other people.

MANNERS: A clearer understanding.

JUDY: I didn't mean that.

MANNERS: Yale, please!

(All silent.)

I placed an option on this script so fast . . .

(Sheldon raises his hand.)

I tied it up, Sheldon, so that no one else could get hold of it. When I showed it to Hoskins . . .

WILETTA *(To Sheldon)*: The producer. Another nice man.

MANNERS: Well, the rest is history. This is my first Broadway show . . .

(Applause from cast.)

But I definitely know what I want and however unorthodox my methods, I promise never to bore you.

SHELDON *(Popping his fingers rapidly)*: He's like that.

MANNERS: I bring to this a burning desire above and beyond anything I've . . . well, I'm ready to sweat blood. I want to see you kids drawing pay envelopes for a long time to come and . . .

(Sheldon applauds; the others join him. Sheldon aims his remark at Millie.)

SHELDON: Listen to the man! Listen.

(Manners holds up his hand for silence.)

MANNERS: At ease. *(Mainly for John and Judy)* I ask this, please forget your old methods of work and go along with me. I'll probably confuse the hell out of you for the first few days, but after that . . . well, I hope we'll be swingin'. Now, you're all familiar with the story . . .

WILETTA: Oh, I never had anything affect me so much in all my life.

ALL *(Ad-lib)*: There was one part . . . I have a question . . . Uh-huh . . . A question . . .

MANNERS: We will not discuss the parts.

(*John groans in mock agony.*)

JUDY: One little thing.
MANNERS: We will *not* discuss the parts.

(*Eddie smiles knowingly.*)

We will not read the play down from beginning to end.
SHELDON (*Popping his fingers*): There he goes!
MANNERS: We will *not* delve into character backgrounds . . . not now. Turn to Act 1, Scene 2, page fifteen.

(*Actors scramble madly for places in scripts.*)

Top of the page. Eddie, you read for O'Wray. Judy! Stand up!

(*Judy stands hesitantly while Manners toys with a sheet of paper.*)

Walk downstage!

(*Judy is startled and nervous, she walks upstage. The others are eager to correct her but Manners will not tolerate cast interference. He crumbles the paper, throws it to the floor, takes Judy by the shoulders, and speedily leads her around the stage.*)

Downstage! Center stage! Left center! Right center! Up right! Up left, down center, down right, down left, upstage . . . DOWNSTAGE!
JUDY: I know, I forgot . . .
MANNERS: Don't forget again. Take downstage.

(*Manners notices the paper he threw on the floor.*)

A trashy stage is most distracting.

(Judy starts to pick up the paper.)

Hold your position! Wiletta, pick up the paper!

(John and Sheldon start for the paper.)

I asked Wiletta! *(Catching Wiletta's eye)* Well?

WILETTA *(Shocked into a quick flare of temper)*: Well, hell! I ain't the damn janitor! *(Trying to check her temper)* I . . . well, I . . . shucks . . . I . . . damn.

(Even though Manners was trying to catch them off guard, he didn't expect this.)

MANNERS: Cut! Cut! It's all over.

(Everyone is surprised again.)

What you have just seen is . . . is . . . is fine acting.

(He is quite shaken and embarrassed from Wiletta's action.)

Actors struggle for weeks to do what you have done perfectly . . . the first time. You gave me anger, frustration, movement, er . . . excitement. Your faces were alive! Why? You did what came naturally, you believed . . . That is the quality I want in your work . . . the firm texture of truth.

JUDY: Oh, you tricked us.

MILLIE: I didn't know what to think.

JOHN: Tension all over the place.

(Wiletta is still having a hard time getting herself under control. She fans herself with a pocket handkerchief and tries to muster a weak laugh.)

WILETTA: Yes indeed.

(Manners gingerly touches Wiletta and shivers in mock fear.)

MANNERS: She plays rough. "Well, hell!" Honey, I love you, believe me.

SHELDON: Oh, she cut up!

(Wiletta tries to laugh along with them, but it's hard going. From this point on, she watches Manners with a sharp eye, always cautious and on the lookout.)

WILETTA: Yes . . . well, let's don't play that no more.

MANNERS: Top of the page. Judy, you're appealing to your father to allow some of his tenant farmers . . .

(He glances at script to find the next direction. Sheldon leans over and whispers to Wiletta.)

WILETTA: Sharecroppers.

SHELDON: Oh.

MANNERS: . . . hold a barn dance. Now! Some of them have been talking about voting.

SHELDON: Trouble.

MANNERS *(Points first to Millie, then Wiletta)*: Petunia and Ruby are in your father's study . . . er . . . er . . .

(Manners consults script again.)

SHELDON *(Without consulting script)*: Cleanin' up. Sure, that's what they're doin'.

MANNERS: Tidying up. Your father is going over his account books, you're there . . .

SHELDON *(With admiration)*: Lookin' pretty.

MANNERS: There's an awful echo coming from our assistant director.

SHELDON *(Laughs)*: 'Sistant director! This man breaks me up all the time!

MANNERS *(Liking the salve)*: What, what did you say?

SHELDON: Say you tickle me to death.

WILETTA: Tickles me too.

MANNERS: Take it!

JUDY *(Reading)*: Papa, it's a good year, isn't it?

EDDIE *(With a too-broad Southern accent)*: I'd say fair, fair to middlin'.

(Cast snickers.)

MANNERS: All right, Barrymore, just read it.

JUDY: Papa, it's Petunia's birthday today.

EDDIE: That so? Happy birthday, Petunia.

MILLIE *(Wearily)*: Thank you, sir.

MANNERS *(Correcting the reading)*: You feel good, full of ginger . . . your birthday!

MILLIE *(Remembers the old, standard formula; gives the line with a chuckle and extra warmth)*: Thank you, sir.

JUDY: It would be nice if they could have a stomp in the barn.

MILLIE *(Her attitude suggesting that Judy thought up the line)*: Hmmph.

EDDIE: No need to have any barn stomp until this election business is over.

MILLIE: What the hell is a stomp?

JUDY: I can't see why.

MANNERS: A barn dance. You know that, Millie.

EDDIE: Ruby, you think y'all oughta use the barn?

WILETTA *(Pleasantly)*: Lord, have mercy, Mr. Renard, don't ask me 'cause I don't know nothin'.

EDDIE: Well, better forget about it.

JUDY: Oh, Papa, let the . . . let the . . .

MILLIE *(For Judy's benefit)*: Mmmmmmmmmmph. Why didn't they call it a barn dance?

JUDY: . . . let the . . . *(Stops reading)* Oh, must I say that word?

MANNERS: What word?

MILLIE: *Darkies.* That's the word. It says, "Papa, let the darkies have their fun."

MANNERS: *What* do you want to say?

MILLIE: She could say . . . "Let *them* have their fun."

MANNERS: But that's Carrie. *(To Sheldon)* Do you object?

SHELDON: Well, no, not if that's how they spoke in them days.

MANNERS: The time is now, down South in some remote little county, they say those things . . . now. Can you object in an artistic sense?

SHELDON: No, but you better ask him, he's more artistic than I am.

JOHN: No, I don't object. I don't like the word but it is used, it's a slice of life. Let's face it, Judy wouldn't use it, Mr. Manners wouldn't . . .

MANNERS *(Very pleased with John's answer)*: Call me Al, everybody. Al's good enough, Johnny.

JOHN: Al wouldn't say it but Carrie would.

(Manners gives Wiletta an inquiring look.)

WILETTA: Lord, have mercy, don't ask me 'cause I don't know . . .

(She stops short as she realizes that she is repeating words from the script. She's disturbed that she's repeating the exact line the author indicated.

Manners gives Judy a light tap on the head.)

MANNERS: Yale! Proceed.

EDDIE *(Reads)*: Ruby and Petunia leave the room and wait on the porch.

JUDY: Please, Papa, I gave my word. I ask one little thing and . . .

EDDIE: All right! Before you know it, them niggers will be runnin' me!

JUDY: Please don't use that word!

MANNERS: Oh, stop it!

WILETTA: That's her line in the play, Mr. Manners, Carrie says . . .

ALL: Please, don't use the word.

(Manners signals Eddie to carry on.)

EDDIE *(Reads)*: Carrie runs out to the porch.

JUDY: You can use the barn!

MILLIE: Lord, have mercy . . .

EDDIE *(Intones)*: Wrong line.

MILLIE *(Quickly corrects line)*: Er . . . er, somethin' seems to trouble my spirit, a troublous feelin' is in old Petunia's breast. *(Stops reading) Old* Petunia?

WILETTA: Yes, *old* Petunia!

JUDY *(Reads)*: I'm going upstairs to lay out my white organdy dress.

WILETTA: No, you ain't, I'm gonna do that for you.

JUDY: Then I'll take a nap.

MILLIE: No, you ain't, I'm gonna do that for you.

EDDIE: Wrong line.

MILLIE: Sorry. *(Corrects line)* Yes, child, you rest yourself, you had a terrible hard day. Bless your soul, you just one of God's golden-haired angels.

(Manners is frantically searching for that certain quality. He thinks everything will open once they hit the right chord.)

MANNERS: Cut! Top of page three, Act 1, as it's written. Ruby is shelling beans on the back porch as her son Job approaches.

JOHN: If I can read over . . .

MANNERS: Do as I ask, do it. Take it, Wiletta.

SHELDON (*Popping his fingers*): He's just like that.

WILETTA (*Reads*): Boy, where you goin'?

JOHN: Down to Turner's Corner.

WILETTA: You ain't lost nothin' down there. Turner and his brother is talkin' 'bout votin'. I know.

JOHN: They only talkin', I'm goin'.

SHELDON: Mr. Renard say to stay outta that.

JOHN: I got a letter from the president 'bout goin' in the army, Turner says when that happens, a man's s'posed to vote and things.

(*Millie and Judy are very pleased about this line.*)

SHELDON: Letter ain't from no president, it come from the crackers on the draft board.

JOHN: It *say* from the president.

WILETTA: Pa say you don't go.

(*Manners is jotting down a flood of notes.*)

JOHN: Sorry, but I say I'd be there.

SHELDON: I don't know who that boy take after.

EDDIE: Ruby dashes from the porch and Sam follows her. Carrie comes outside and Renard follows her.

(*Eddie reads Renard.*)

You pamper them rascals too much, see how they do? None of 'em's worth their weight in salt, that boy would steal the egg out of a cake.

(*Judy tries to laugh, while Millie watches coldly. Manners is amazed at the facial distortion.*)

JUDY: It says laugh.

MANNERS: Well?

JUDY *(Laughs and continues reading)*: But I can't help feeling sorry for them, they didn't ask to be born.

MILLIE *(Just loud enough for Judy's ears)*: Hmmmmmmph.

JUDY: I keep thinking, there but for the grace of God go I. If we're superior we should prove it by our actions.

SHELDON *(Commenting on the line)*: There you go, prove it!

(Manners is taking more notes. Judy is disturbed by the reactions to her reading. She hesitates. Manners looks up. The phone rings. Eddie goes off to answer.)

JUDY: She *is* their friend, right? It's just that I feel reactions and . . .

MANNERS: What reactions?

MILLIE: I was reacting.

MANNERS: Ohhhhh, who pays Millie any attention, that's her way.

MILLIE: There you go.

SHELDON: Sure is.

JUDY *(Tries again but she's very uncomfortable)*: I . . . I keep thinking . . . there but for the grace of God . . .

MANNERS: Are you planning to cry?

JUDY: No, but . . . no.

(She's fighting to hold back the tears.)

SHELDON: Millie's pickin' on her.

MANNERS: Utter nonsense!

JUDY: My part seems . . . she seems so smug.

MILLIE *(To Sheldon)*: Keep my name out of your mouth.

WILETTA *(To Sheldon)*: Mind your business, your own affairs.

MANNERS: This is fantastic. What in the hell is smug?

(Henry enters with a cardboard box full of coffee containers and a large paper bag.)

Cut! Coffee break! *(To Judy)* Especially you.

HENRY: Told the waiter feller to fix up everything nice.

MANNERS *(Looks in bag)*: What's this?

HENRY: That's what you said. I heard you. "Jelly doughnuts!" you said.

(Sheldon gets a container of coffee for Judy and one for himself.)

MANNERS: I won't eat it!

HENRY: But I heard you.

MANNERS: Take your coffee and leave.

(Henry starts to leave without the coffee.)

Don't play games, take it with you.

(Henry snatches a container and leaves in a quiet huff. Sheldon hands coffee to Judy, but Millie snatches it from his hand.)

MILLIE: I know you brought that for me.

MANNERS: Where do they find these characters? All right, he's old but it's an imposition . . . he's probably ninety, you know.

WILETTA *(Laughs and then suddenly stops)*: We all get old sometimes.

(Eddie hurries onstage; looks worried.)

EDDIE: It's Mrs. Manners . . . she . . . she says it's urgent. She has to talk to you *now* . . . immediately.

MANNERS: Oh, you stupid jerk. Why did you say I was here? You and your big, stupid mouth. Couldn't you say, "He isn't here now, I'll give him your message"?

EDDIE: I'm sorry. She was so . . . so . . . Well, she said right off, "I *know* he's there." If I had any idea that she would . . .

MANNERS: I don't expect you to have *ideas!* Only common sense, just a little common sense. Where do you find a stage manager these days?

EDDIE: I can tell her you can't be disturbed now.

MANNERS: No, numbskull, don't do another thing, you've done enough. *(With wry humor)* Alimony is not enough, every time I make three extra dollars she takes me to court to get two-thirds of it. If I don't talk to her I'll have a subpoena. You're stupid.

(He exits to the telephone. During the brief silence that follows, Eddie is miserably self-conscious.)

WILETTA *(Tries to save the day)*: Well . . . I'm glad it's getting a little like winter now. We sure had a hot summer. Did you have a nice summer?

EDDIE *(Choking back his suppressed anger)*: I worked in stock . . . summer theater. It was okay.

WILETTA: That's nice. What did you do?

EDDIE *(Relaxing more)*: Kind of jack-of-all-trades . . . understudied some, stage-managed, made sets . . .

MILLIE: And did three people out of a job.

JUDY: I spent the summer with my folks. Soon as we open, I want everyone to come up to Bridgeport and have a glorious day!

(Manners returns, looks up briefly.)

Daddy makes the yummiest barbecue, you'll love it.

WILETTA: You better discuss it with your folks first.

JUDY: Why?

MILLIE: 'Cause we wouldn't want it discussed after we got there.

SHELDON: No, thank you, ma'am. I'm plannin' to be busy all winter lookin' for an apartment, I sure hate roomin'.

EDDIE: I have my own apartment. It's only a cold-water walk-up but I have it fixed real nice like the magazines show you . . . whitewashed brick and mobiles hanging in the kitchen and living room. I painted the floors black and spattered them with red and white paint . . . I learned that in stock . . . then I shellacked over it and waxed it . . . and I scraped all of the furniture down to the natural wood . . .

MILLIE: Oh, hush, you're making me tired. Cold-water flat!

EDDIE: It gives a cheery effect . . .

MILLIE: And it'll give you double pneumonia.

SHELDON: Yeah, that's the stuff you got to watch.

EDDIE: Well, it's only thirty dollars a month.

SHELDON: They got any colored livin' in that buildin'?

EDDIE: I . . . I . . . I don't know. I haven't seen any.

SHELDON: Well, there's none there then.

EDDIE *(Slightly ill at ease)*: Sheldon, I'll gladly ask.

SHELDON *(In great alarm)*: Oh, no, no, no! I don't want to be the first.

MILLIE: Damn cold-water flats! I like ease, comfort, furs, cards, big, thick steaks. I want everything.

EDDIE *(Trying to change the subject)*: Aren't there a lot of new shows this season?

JUDY: My mother says . . . gosh, every time I open my mouth it's something about my parents. It's not stylish to love your parents . . . you either have a mother-complex or a father-fixation!

(She laughs and Manners looks up again. He doesn't care for her remarks.)

But I'm crazy about my parents, but then maybe that's abnormal. I probably have a mother-father-fixation.

WILETTA: What did your mother say?

JUDY: "Never have limitations on your horizon, reach for infinity!" She also feels that everyone has a right to an equal education and not separate either.

JOHN: She sounds like a wonderful woman who . . .

JUDY *(Raising her voice)*: Oh, I get so mad about this prejudice nonsense! It's a wonder colored people don't go out and *kill* somebody, I mean actually, really do it . . . bloody murder, you know?

SHELDON: There's lotsa folks worse off than we are, Millie.

MILLIE: Well, all I hope is that they don't like it, dontcha know.

MANNERS *(Boastful about his trials and troubles)*: The seven-year-old kid, the seven-year-old kid . . . to hear her tell it, our son is ragged, barefoot, hungry . . . and his teeth are lousy. The orthodontist says he needs braces . . . they wanta remake his mouth. The kid is falling to pieces. When I go for visitation . . . he looks in my pockets before he says hello. Can you imagine? Seven years old. The orthodontist and the psychiatrist . . . the story of my life. But he's a bright kid . . . smart as a whip . . . you can't fool him. *(A big sigh)* Oh, well, let's go. Suppose you were all strangers, had never heard anything about this story except the snatches you heard today. What would you know?

MILLIE: It's my birthday.

(Wiletta is following him closely; she doesn't care to be caught off guard again.)

JOHN: Carrie's father has tenant farmers working for him.

MANNERS: Yes and . . .

JUDY: They want to hold a barn dance and he's against it because . . .

JOHN: Some of the Negroes are planning to vote for the first time and there's opposition . . .

SHELDON: His ma and pa don't want him mixed in it 'cause they smell trouble.

JUDY: And my father overheard that John is in it.

SHELDON: And *he don't like it*, that's another thing.

WILETTA (*Amazed that they have learned so much*): Mmmmmmm, all of that.

JOHN: But Job is determined.

JUDY: And he's been notified by the draft board.

SHELDON: And the paper, the paper!

MANNERS: Paper?

WILETTA: You know, upstage, downstage, and doin' what comes natural.

MANNERS: Not bad for an hour's work.

EDDIE: Amazing.

SHELDON (*Popping his fingers*): Man is on the ball. Fast.

MANNERS: Now we can see how we're heading for the lynching.

SHELDON (*Starts to peep at back page of script*): Lynchin'?

MANNERS: We're dealing with an anti-lynch theme. I want it uncluttered, clear in your mind, you must see the skeleton framework within which we're working. Wiletta, turn to the last page of Act 1.

EDDIE: Fifty.

MANNERS: Wiletta, dear heart . . . the end of the act finds you alone on the porch, worried, heartsick . . .

WILETTA: And singin' a song, sittin', worryin', and singin'.

MANNERS: It's not simply a song, it's a summing up. You're thinking of Renard, the threats, the people and your son . . .

(*Wiletta is tensely listening, trying to follow him. Manners stands behind her and gently shakes her shoulders.*)

Loosen up, let the thoughts flood over you. I know you have to read . . .

WILETTA: Oh, I know the song, learned it when I was a child.

MANNERS: Hold a thought, close your eyes, and think aloud . . . get a good start and then sing . . . speak your mind and then sing.

WILETTA *(Not for thinking out loud)*: I know exactly what you want.

MANNERS: Blurt out the first thing that enters your mind.

WILETTA *(Sings a mournful dirge of despair)*: Come and go with me to that land, come and go with me to that land . . .

MANNERS: Gosh, that guy can write.

WILETTA:

>Come and go with me to that land where I'm bound
>No confusion in that land, no confusion in that land
>No confusion in that land where I'm bound . . .

MILLIE *(Wipes her eyes)*: A heartbreaker.

EDDIE: Oh, Wiletta, it's so . . . so . . . gosh.

JOHN: Leaves you weak.

MANNERS: Beautiful. What were you thinking?

WILETTA *(Ready to move on to something else)*: Thank you.

MANNERS: What were you thinking?

WILETTA: I thought . . . I . . . er, er . . . I don't know, whatever you said.

MANNERS: Tell me. You're not a vacuum, you thought something.

JOHN: Your motivation. What motivated . . .

MANNERS *(Waving John out of it)*: You thought *something*, right?

WILETTA: Uh-huh.

MANNERS: And out of the thought came song.

WILETTA: Yeah.

MANNERS: What did you think?

WILETTA: I thought that's what you wanted.

(She realizes she is the center of attention and finds it uncomfortable.)

MANNERS: It won't do. You must know why you do a thing, that way you're true to me, to the part, and yourself . . .

WILETTA: Didn't you like it?

MANNERS: Very much but . . . I'm sure you've never worked this way before, but you're not carrying a tray or answering doorbells, this is substance, meat. I demand that you *know* what you're doing and *why*, at all times, I will accept nothing less.

WILETTA *(To John and Judy)*: I know, you have to justify.

SHELDON *(Worried and trying to help Wiletta)*: You was thinkin' how sad it was, wasn't you?

WILETTA: Uh-huh.

MANNERS: It's new to you but it must be done. Let go, think aloud and when you are moved to do so . . . sing.

(Wiletta looks blank.)

Start anywhere.

WILETTA: Ah, er . . . it's so sad that folks can't vote . . . it's also sad that er, er . . .

MANNERS: No.

(Manners picks up newspaper.)

We'll try word association. I'll give you a word, then you say what comes to your mind and keep on going . . . one word brings on another . . . Montgomery!

WILETTA: Alabama.

MANNERS: Montgomery!

WILETTA: Alabama.

MANNERS: Montgomery!

WILETTA: Reverend King is speakin' on Sunday.

MANNERS: Colored.

WILETTA: Lights changin' colors all around me.

MANNERS: Colored.

WILETTA: They . . . they . . .

MANNERS: Colored.

WILETTA: "They got any colored in that buildin'?"

MANNERS: Children, little children.

WILETTA: Children . . . children . . . "Pick up that paper!" Oh, my . . .

MANNERS: Lynching.

WILETTA: Killin'! Killin'!

MANNERS: Killing.

WILETTA: It's the man's theater, the man's money, so what you gonna do?

MANNERS: Oh, Wiletta . . . I don't know! *Darkness!*

WILETTA: A star! Oh, I can't, I don't like it . . .

MANNERS: Sing.

WILETTA *(Sings a song of strength and anger)*:
    Come and go with me to that land

(The song is overpowering; we see a woman who could fight the world.)

    Come and go with me to that land
    Come and go with me to that land—
    Where I'm bound.

JUDY: Bravo! Magnificent!

MANNERS: Wiletta, if you dare! You will undo us! Are you out of your senses? When you didn't know what you were doing . . . perfection on the nose. I'll grant you the first interpretation was right, without motivating. All right, I'll settle for that.

WILETTA *(Feeling very lost)*: I said I *knew* what you wanted.

MANNERS: Judy! I . . . I want to talk to you about . . . about Carrie.

(He rises and starts for the dressing room.)

Eddie, will you dash out and get me a piece of danish?
Okay, at ease.

(Eddie quickly exits. Manners and Judy exit stage right toward dressing rooms.)

MILLIE *(To John)*: Look, don't get too close to her.

SHELDON: Mind your own business.

JOHN: What have I done?

MILLIE: You're too friendly with her.

WILETTA: Justify. Ain't enough to do it, you got to justify.

JOHN: I've only been civil.

MILLIE: That's too friendly.

WILETTA: Got a splittin' headache.

SHELDON *(To Wiletta)*: I wish I had an aspirin for you.

MILLIE *(To John)*: All set to run up and see her folks. Didn't you
hear her say they expect something terrible to happen to
her? Well, you're one of the terrible things they have in
mind!

SHELDON: Mind your business.

MILLIE: It is my business. When they start raisin' a fund for his
defense, they're gonna come and ask me for money and I'll
have to be writin' the president and signin' petitions . . . so
it's my business.

SHELDON: I tell you, son. I'm friendly with white folks in a distant
sorta way but I don't get too close. Take Egypt, Russia, all
these countries, why they kickin' up their heels? 'Cause of
white folks, I wouldn't trust one of 'em sittin' in front of me
on a merry-go-round, wouldn't trust 'em if they was laid up
in bed with lockjaw and the mumps both at the same time.

JOHN: Last time I heard from you, you said it was the colored
who made all the trouble.

SHELDON: They do, they're the worst ones. There's two kinda people that's got the world messed up for good, that's the colored and the white, and I got no use for either one of 'em.

MILLIE: I'm going to stop trying to help people.

JOHN: Hell, I'm through with it. Oh, I'm learning the ropes!

SHELDON: *That's* why they don't do more colored shows . . . troublemakers, potboilers, spoon stirrers . . . and sharper than a serpent's tooth! Colored women wake up in the mornin' with their fists ball up . . . ready to fight.

WILETTA: What in the devil is all this justifyin'? Ain't necessary.

MILLIE *(To Sheldon)*: And you crawlin' all over me to hand her coffee! Damn "Tom."

SHELDON: You talkin' 'bout your relatives, ain't talkin' 'bout me, if I'm a "Tom," you a "Jemima."

JOHN: I need out, I need air.

(He exits stage left.)

SHELDON: White folks is stickin' together, stickin' together, stickin' together . . . we fightin'.

WILETTA: Hush, I got a headache.

MILLIE: I need a breath of air, too, before I slap the taste out of somebody's mouth.

(Millie grabs her coat and exits stage left.)

SHELDON: I hope the wind blows her away. They gonna kick us until we all out in the street . . . unemployed . . . get all the air you want then. Sometimes I take low, yes, gotta take low. Man says somethin' to me, I say . . . "Yes, sure, certainly." You 'n' me know how to do. That ain't *Tommin'*, that's common sense. You and me . . . we don't mind takin' low because we tryin' to accomplish somethin' . . .

WILETTA: I mind . . . I do mind . . . I mind . . . I mind . . .

SHELDON: Well, yeah, we all mind . . . but you got to swaller what you mind. What you mind won't buy beans. I mean, you gotta take what you mind to survive . . . to eat, to breathe . . .

WILETTA *(Tensely)*: *I mind.* Leave me alone.

(Sheldon exits with a sigh. Henry enters carrying a lunch box. Wiletta turns; she looks so distressed.)

HENRY: They've all flown the coop?

WILETTA: Yes.

HENRY: What's the matter? Somebody hurt your feelin's?

WILETTA: Yes.

HENRY: Don't fret, it's too nice a day. I believe in treatin' folks right. When you're just about through with this life, that's the time when you know how to live. Seems like yesterday I was forty years old and the day before that I wasn't but nineteen . . . Think of it.

WILETTA: I don't like to think . . . makes me fightin' mad.

HENRY *(Giving vent to his pent-up feelings)*: Don't I know it? When he yelled about jelly doughnuts, I started to land one on him! Oh, I almost did it!

WILETTA: I know it!

HENRY: But . . . "Hold your temper!" I says. I have a most ferocious temper.

WILETTA: Me too. I take and take, then watch out!

HENRY: Have to hold my temper, I don't want to kill the man.

WILETTA: Yeah, makes you feel like fightin'.

HENRY *(Joining in the spirit of the discussion)*: Sure I'm a fighter and I come from a fightin' people.

WILETTA: You from Ireland?

HENRY: A fightin' people! Didn't we fight for the home rule?

WILETTA: Uh-huh, now you see there.

(Wiletta doesn't worry about making sense out of Henry's speech on Ireland; it's the feeling behind it that counts.)

HENRY: Oh, a history of great men, fightin' men!

WILETTA *(Rallying to the call, she answers as though sitting on an amen bench at a revival meeting)*: Yes, carry on.

HENRY: Ah, yes, we was fightin' for the home rule! Ah, there was some great men!

WILETTA: I know it.

HENRY: There was Parnell! Charles Stewart Parnell!

WILETTA: All right!

HENRY: A figure of a man! The highest! Fightin' hard for the home rule! A parliamentarian! And they clapped him in the blasted jailhouse for six months!

WILETTA: Yes, my Lord!

HENRY: And Gladstone introduced the bill . . . and later on you had Dillon and John Redmond . . . and then when the home rule was almost put through, what did you think happened? World War One! That killed the whole business!

WILETTA *(Very indignant)*: Oh, if it ain't one thing, it's another!

HENRY: I'm descended from a great line! And then the likes of him with his jelly doughnuts! Jelly doughnuts, indeed, is it? What does he know? Tramplin' upon a man's dignity! Me father was the greatest, most dignified man you've ever seen . . . and he played vaudeville! Oh, the bearin' of him! *(Angrily demonstrating his father's dignity)* Doin' the little soft-shoe step . . . and it's take your hat off to the ladies . . . and step along there . . .

WILETTA: Henry, I want to be an actress. I've always wanted to be an actress and they ain't gonna do me the way they did the home rule! I want to be an actress 'cause one day you're nineteen and then forty and so on . . . I want to be an actress! Henry, they stone us when we try to go to school, the world's crazy.

HENRY: It's a shame, a shame . . .

WILETTA: Where the hell do I come in? Every damn body pushin' me off the face of the earth! I want to be an actress . . . hell, I'm gonna be one, you hear me?

(She pounds the table.)

HENRY: Sure, and why not, I'd like to know!

WILETTA *(Quietly)*: Yes, damnit . . . and why not? Why in the hell not?

(Blues record in; woman singer.)

Act 2

*The theater. Ten o'clock Thursday morning. Blues music in, up and out.
Furniture has been changed around; some of the old set removed.*

*Bill O'Wray, a character actor (white), stands upstage on a makeshift
platform. He radiates strength and power as he addresses an imaginary
audience. Manners stands stage left, tie loosened, hair ruffled. He is
hepped up with nervous energy, can barely stand still. Eddie is stage
right, in charge of the script and a tape recorder; he follows the script
and turns up the tape recorder on cue from Manners. Bill is delivering
a "masterful" rendition of Renard's speech on "tolerance." Manners
is elated one moment, deflated the next. Eddie is obviously nervous,
drawn, and lacking the easygoing attitude of Act 1.*

BILL *(Intones speech with vigor and heartfelt passion)*: My friends, if
   all the world were just, there would be no need for valor . . .
   And those of us who are of a moderate mind . . . I would say
   the majority . . . *(Light applause from tape recorder)* . . . we are
   anything but lighthearted. But the moving finger writes and
   having writ moves *on*. No you can't wash out a word of it.
   Heretofore we've gotten along with our Nigra population

. . . but times change. *(Applause from tape recorder)* I do not argue with any man who believes in segregation. I, of all people, will not, cannot question that belief. We all believe in the words of Henry Clay: "Sir, I would rather be right than be president."

(Eddie sleeps his cue.)

MANNERS: Damnit! Eddie!

(Eddie suddenly switches to loud applause.)

BILL: But difficulties are things that show what men are, and necessity is still the mother of invention. As Emerson so aptly pointed out: "The true test of civilization is not the— census, nor the size of cities, nor the crops—but the kind of man the country turns out." Oh, my friends, let every man look before he leaps, let us consider submitting to the present evil lest a greater one befall us—say to yourself, my honor is dearer to me than my life. *(Very light applause)* I say moderation—for these are the times that try men's souls! In these terrible days we must realize—how oft the darkest hour of ill breaks brightest into dawn. Moderation, yes. *(Very light applause)* Even the misguided, infamous Adolph Hitler said: "One should guard against believing the great masses to be more stupid than they actually are!" *(Applause)* Oh, friends, moderation. Let us weigh our answer very carefully when the dark-skinned Oliver Twist approaches our common pot and says: "Please, sir, I want some more." When we say: "No," remember that a soft answer turneth away wrath. Ohhh, we shall come out of the darkness, and sweet is pleasure after pain. If we are superior, let us show our superiority!

(Manners directs Eddie to take applause up high and then out.)

Moderation. With wisdom and moderation, these terrible days will pass. I am reminded of the immortal words of Longfellow:

> And the night shall be filled with music,
>   And the cares, that infest the day,
> Shall fold their tents, like the Arabs,
>   And as silently steal away.

(Terrific applause. Manners slaps Bill on his back, dashes to Eddie, and turns the applause up and down.)

MANNERS: Is this such a Herculean task? All you have to do is listen! Inattention—aggravates the hell out of me!

(When Bill drops out of character we see that he is very different from the strong Renard. He appears to be worried at all times. He has a habit of negatively shaking his head even though nothing is wrong. Bill O'Wray is but a shadow of a man—but by some miracle he turns into a dynamic figure as Renard. As Bill—he sees dragons in every corner and worries about each one.)

BILL: I don't know, I don't know . . .

(Manners fears the worst for the show as he watches Bill.)

MANNERS: What? What is it?
BILL *(Half dismissing the thought)*: Oh, well . . . I guess . . .

(Eddie is toying with the machine and turns the applause up by accident.)

MANNERS: Hello, Eddie, a little consideration! Why do you do it? Damned childish!

(Eddie turns off machine.)

What's bothering you?

BILL: Well, you never can tell . . . but I don't know . . .

MANNERS: Bill, cut it out, come on.

BILL: That Arab stuff . . . you know, quietly folding his tent . . . you're gonna get a laugh . . . and then on the other hand you might offend somebody . . . well, we'll see . . .

MANNERS: Eddie, make a note of that. Arab folding his tent. I'll take it up with Bronson.

(Eddie is making notes.)

BILL: I'm tellin' you, you don't need it . . . wouldn't lose a thing . . . the Longfellow quote . . . I don't know, maybe I'm wrong but . . .

MANNERS: You act like you've lost your last friend! I'm the one holding the blasted bag!

(Bill takes Show Business Weekly *out of his coat pocket.)*

BILL: Well, maybe I shouldn't have said . . .

MANNERS: I'm out of my mind! When I think of the money borrowed and for what! Oh, I'm just talking. This always happens when the ship leaves port. The union's making me take three extra stagehands *(Laughs)* . . . They hate *us*! Co-produce, filthy word! You know who I had to put the bite on for an extra ten thousand? My ex-wife's present boyfriend. Enough to emasculate a man for the rest of his life!

BILL: How is Fay? Sweet kid. I was sure surprised when you two broke it off. Oh, well, that's the way . . .

MANNERS: She's fine and we're good friends. Thank God for civilization.

BILL: That's nice. Ten thousand? She must have connected up with a big wheel, huh?

MANNERS: I've known you long enough to ask a favor.

BILL: All depends.

MANNERS: Will you stop running off at lunch hour? It looks bad.

BILL: Now, wait a minute . . .

EDDIE: I eat with them all the time.

MANNERS: Drop it, Eddie. Unity in *this* company is very important. Hell, I don't care, but it looks like you don't want to eat with the colored members of the cast.

BILL: I don't.

EDDIE: I guess you heard him.

MANNERS: Bill, this is fantastic. I never credited you with this kind of . . . silly, childlike . . .

BILL: There's not a prejudiced bone in my body. It is important that I eat my lunch. I used to have an ulcer. I have nothing against anybody but I can't eat my damn lunch . . . people *stare*. They sit there glaring and staring.

MANNERS: Nonsense.

BILL: Tuesday I lunched with Millie because I bumped into her on the street. That restaurant . . . people straining and looking at me as if I were an old lecher! God knows what they're thinking. I've got to eat my lunch. After all . . . I can't stand that . . .

MANNERS *(Laughs)*: All right but mix a little . . . it's the show . . . do it for the show.

BILL: Every time I open my mouth somebody is telling me don't say this or that . . . Millie doesn't want to be called "gal" . . . I call *all* women "gal" . . . I don't know . . . I'm not going into analysis about this . . . I'm not. How do you think my character is shaping up?

MANNERS: Great, no complaints . . . fine.

(Wiletta drags in, tired and worn.)

'Morning, sweetie.

EDDIE: Good morning.

WILETTA *(Indicating script)*: I been readin' this back and forth and over again.

MANNERS *(Automatic sympathy)*: Honey, don't . . .

WILETTA: My neighbor, Miss Green, she come up and held the book and I sat there justifyin' like you said . . .

MANNERS: Darling, don't think. You're great until you start thinking. I don't expect you to . . .

WILETTA *(Weak laugh)*: I've been in this business a long time, more than twenty-five years and . . .

MANNERS: Don't tell it, you're beautiful.

WILETTA: Guess I can do like the others. We was justifyin' and Miss Green says to me . . .

BILL *(Gets in his good deed)*: Wiletta, you look wonderful, you really do.

WILETTA: Huh?

BILL: You . . . you're looking well.

WILETTA: Thank you, Miss Green says . . .

MANNERS *(Wearily)*: Oh, a plague on Miss Green. Darling, it's too early to listen to outside criticism, it can be dangerous if the person doesn't understand . . .

WILETTA: Miss Green puts on shows at the church . . . and she had an uncle that was a sharecropper, so she says the first act . . .

MANNERS *(Flips the script to Act 3)*: We're hitting the third today.

WILETTA: Miss Green also conducts the church choir . . .

MANNERS: Wiletta, don't complicate my life. *(To Bill and Eddie)* Isn't she wonderful? *(To Wiletta)* Dear heart, I adore you.

WILETTA *(Feels like a fool as she limply trails on)*: She . . . she did the *Messiah* . . . Handel's *Messiah* . . . last Easter . . . and folks come from downtown to hear it . . . all kinds of folks . . . white folks too.

MANNERS: Eddie! Did I leave the schedule at home?

(Eddie hands him the schedule.)

EDDIE: I have a copy.

WILETTA: Miss Green says, now . . . she said it . . . she says the third act doesn't justify with the first . . . no, wait . . . her exact words was, "The third act is not the natural outcome of the first." I thought, I thought she might be right.

MANNERS *(Teasing)*: Make me a solemn promise, don't start thinking.

(Sheldon enters in a rush and hastily begins to remove scarves, coat, etc.)

SHELDON: Good mornin', there ain't no justice.

(Bill O'Wray glances at Show Business *from time to time.)*

EDDIE: What a greeting.

SHELDON: I dreamed six, twelve, six, one, two . . . just like that. You know what come out yesterday? Six, one, three. What you gonna do?

MANNERS: Save your money.

BILL: Hey, what do you know?

MANNERS: Did we make the press?

SHELDON *(To Wiletta)*: Friend of mine died yesterday, went to see about his apartment . . . gone! Just like that!

BILL: Gary Brewer's going into rehearsal on *Lost and Lonely*.

MANNERS: Been a long time.

BILL: He was in that Hollywood investigation some years ago.

SHELDON *(To Eddie)*: They musta applied whilst the man was dyin'.

MANNERS: He wasn't really in it, someone named him I think.

BILL: You knew him well, didn't you?

MANNERS: Me? I don't know him. I've worked with him a couple of times but I don't really know him.

BILL: A very strange story reached me once, some fellow was planning to name me, can you imagine?

(Millie enters wearing a breathtaking black suit. She is radiant.)

EDDIE: That's ridiculous.

BILL: Nothing ever happened, but that's the story. Naming *me*.

MANNERS *(As he studies schedule)*: Talking about the coast, I could be out there now on a honey of a deal . . . but this I had to do, that's all.

SHELDON: Y'all ever hear my stories 'bout people namin' me?

MANNERS: What?

BILL: Oh, Shel!

(This is a burden Sheldon has carried for quite some time.)

SHELDON: I sang on a program once with Millie, to help some boy that was in trouble . . . but later on I heard they was tryin' to overthrow the gov'ment.

(Manners, Eddie and Bill are embarrassed by this.)

MILLIE: Oh, hush! Your mouth runs like a racehorse!

SHELDON: Well, ain't nothin' wrong with singin' is there? We just sang.

MILLIE *(As she removes her hat)*: A big fool.

MANNERS *(Making peace)*: Oh, now . . . we're all good Americans.

BILL *(To ease the tension)*: I . . . I . . . er, didn't know you went in for singing, Sheldon.

SHELDON: Sure, I even wrote me a coupla tunes. Can make a lotta money like that but you gotta know somebody, I ain't got no pull.

WILETTA *(To Millie)*: He talks too much, talks too much.

MANNERS: Ah, we have a composer, popular stuff?

(Sheldon stands and mechanically rocks to and fro in a rock-and-roll beat as he sings:)

SHELDON:

> You-oo-hoo-oo are my hon-honey
> Ooo-oo-ooo-oo, you smile is su-hu-hunny
> My hu-hu-hunny, bay-hay-hay-bee-e-e-e-e

. . . and it goes like that.

MANNERS: Well!

SHELDON: Thank you.

BILL: I don't know why you haven't sold it, that's all you hear.

(Sheldon is pleased with Bill's compliment but also a little worried.)

MILLIE: Hmmmmmph.

EDDIE: Really a tune.

SHELDON *(To Bill)*: My song . . . it . . . it's copyrighted.

BILL: Oh?

SHELDON: I got papers.

MILLIE *(Extends her wrist to Wiletta)*: Look. My husband is in off the road.

WILETTA: What's the matter?

MILLIE: A new watch, and I got my suit out . . . brought me this watch. We looked at a freezer this morning . . . food freezer . . . what's best, a chest freezer or an upright? I don't know.

(Judy enters dressed a little older than in Act 1; her hair is set with more precision. She is reaching for a sophistication that can never go deeper than the surface. She often makes graceful, studied postures and tries new attitudes, but very often she forgets.)

JUDY: Greetings and salutations. Sheldon, how are you, dear?

SHELDON: Thank you.

JUDY (*As Millie displays her wrist for inspection*): Millie, darling, how lovely, ohhhhh, exquisite . . .

WILETTA (*Really trying to join in*): Mmmmm, ain't it divine.

(*Henry and John enter together. Henry carries a container of coffee and a piece of danish for Manners. Henry is exact, precise, all business. He carries the container to Manners's table, places pastry, taps Eddie on the shoulder, points to Manners, points to container, nods to Manners and company, turns and leaves, all while dialogue continues. John enters on a cloud. He is drifting more and more toward the heady heights of opportunism. He sees himself on the brink of escaping Wiletta, Millie and Sheldon. It's becoming very easy to conform to Manners's pattern.*)

JOHN: I'm walking in my sleep. I was up all hours last night.

MANNERS: At Sardi's no doubt.

JOHN: No!

JUDY: Exposed! We've found you out.

(*General laughter from Millie, Judy, Bill, Eddie and Manners. Judy is enjoying the intangible joke to the utmost, but as she turns to Wiletta her laughter dies . . . but Wiletta quickly picks it up.*)

WILETTA: Oh, my, yes indeed!

JOHN: I struggled with the third act. I think I won.

(*Millie sticks out her wrist for John's inspection.*)

Exquisite, Millie, beautiful. You deserve it.

(*During the following the conversation tumbles criss-cross in all directions and the only clear things are underscored.*)

MANNERS: Tell him what I told you this morning.

BILL: Why should I swell his head?

MANNERS *(Arm around John's shoulder)*: <u>Hollywood's going to grab you so fast!</u> I won't drop names but our opening night is going to be the end.

MILLIE *(To Wiletta)*: <u>Barbara died!</u>

JUDY *(To Manners)*: Oh, you terrify me!

MILLIE: <u>Died alone in her apartment.</u> Sudden-like!

JOHN: I've got to catch Katherine's performance, I hear it's terrific!

BILL: She's great, only great.

MILLIE: <u>I wouldn't live alone!</u>

MANNERS: She's going to get the award, no doubt about it!

JUDY: Marion Hatterly is good.

MANNERS: Marion is as <u>old as the hills!</u> I mean, she's so old it's embarrassing.

JOHN: But she has a quality.

SHELDON *(To Millie and Wiletta)*: <u>People dyin' like they got nothin' else to do!</u>

JUDY: She has, John, a real quality.

SHELDON: <u>I ain't gonna die</u>, can't afford to do it.

MANNERS: You have to respect her.

EDDIE: Can name her own ticket.

JOHN: Imperishable talent.

MILLIE: <u>Funeral is Monday.</u>

WILETTA *(Weakly, to no one in particular)*: Mmmmm, fascinat-in' . . .

MANNERS: Picnic is over! Third act!

SHELDON: I know my lines.

BILL: Don't worry about lines yet.

MANNERS: No, let him worry . . . I mean it's okay. Beginning of third!

(Wiletta feels dizzy from past conversation. She rises and walks in a half circle, then half circles back again. She is suddenly the center of attraction.)

WILETTA: It . . . it's nighttime and I'm ironin' clothes.

MANNERS: Right. We wander through it. Here's the ironing board, door, window . . . you iron. Carrie is over there crying.

JUDY: Oh, poor, dear, Carrie, crying again.

MANNERS: Petunia is near the window, looking out for Job. Everyone is worried, worried, worried like crazy. Have the lynchers caught Job? Sam is seated in the corner, whittling a stick.

SHELDON *(Flat statement)*: Whittlin' a stick.

MANNERS: Excitement. Everyone knows that a mob is gathering.

(Sheldon is seated and busy running one index finger over the other.)

SHELDON: I'm whittlin' a stick.

MANNERS *(Drumming up excitement)*: The hounds can be heard baying in the distance.

(Sheldon bays to fill in the dog bit. Manners silences him with a gesture.)

Everyone *listens!* They are thinking—has Job been killed? Ruby begins to sing.

(Wiletta begins to sing with a little too much power but Manners directs her down.)

WILETTA: Lord, have mercy, Lord have mercy . . . *(Hums)*

MILLIE *(In abject, big-eyed fear)*: Listen to them dogs in the night.

(Manners warns Sheldon not to provide sound effects.)

WILETTA *(Trying to lose herself in the part)*: Child, you better go now.

(Bill whispers to Eddie.)

EDDIE: *Line. Miss Carrie,* you better go now.
MANNERS: Oh, bother! Don't do that!

(Eddie feels resentful toward Bill as Bill acts as though he had nothing to do with the correction.)

WILETTA: This ain't no place for you to be.

(Judy now plays Carrie in a different way from Act 1. There is a reserved kindliness, rather than real involvement.)

JUDY: I don't want to leave you alone, Ruby.
SHELDON: Thassa mistake, Mr. Manners. She can't be alone if me and Millie is there with her.
MANNERS: Don't interrupt!
SHELDON: Sorry.

(Bill shakes his fist at Sheldon in playful pantomime.)

WILETTA: Man that is born of woman is but a few days and full of trouble.
JUDY: I'm going to drive over to the next county and get my father and Judge Willis.
MILLIE: No, you ain't. Mr. Renard would never forgive me if somethin' was to happen to you.

(Sheldon is very touched and sorry for all concerned as he whittles his stick.)

JUDY: I feel so helpless.
SHELDON *(Interrupts out of sheer frustration)*: Am I still whittlin' the stick?

WILETTA: Damnit, yes.

MANNERS *(Paces to control his annoyance)*: Shel.

SHELDON: I thought I lost my place.

WILETTA *(Picks up Manners's signal)*: Nothin' to do now but pray!

SHELDON *(Recognizes his cue)*: Oh, yeah, that's me. *(Knows his lines almost perfectly)* Lord, once and again and one more time . . .

(Millie moans in the background. Wiletta's mind seems a thousand miles away. Manners snaps his fingers and she begins to moan background for Sheldon's prayer.)

Your humble servant calls on your everlastin' mercy . . .

MILLIE: Yes, Lord!

SHELDON: . . . to beseech, to beseech thy help for all your children this evenin' . . .

MILLIE: This evenin', Lord.

(Manners is busy talking to John.)

SHELDON: But most of all we ask, we pray . . . that you help your son and servant Job . . .

WILETTA: Help him, Lord!

SHELDON *(Doing a grand job of the prayer)*: Walk with Job! Talk with Job! Ohhhhh, be with Job!

JUDY: Yes!

(Manners and Bill give Judy disapproving looks and she clasps her hand over her mouth.)

WILETTA *(Starts to sing and is joined by Sheldon and Millie)*: Death ain't nothin' but a robber, cantcha see, cantcha see . . .

(Manners is in a real tizzy, watching to catch Bill's reaction to the scene, and trying with his whole body to keep the scene up and going.)

MANNERS: Eddie! Direction!

EDDIE: The door opens and Job enters!

WILETTA: Job, why you come here?

(Manners doesn't like her reading. It is too direct and thoughtful.)

MILLIE *(Lashing out)*: They after you! They told you 'bout mixin' in with Turner and that votin'!

MANNERS: Oh, good girl!

WILETTA: I'm the one to talk to my boy!

JOHN *(A frightened, shivering figure)*: If somebody could get me a wagon, I'll take the low road around Simpkin's Hollow and catch a train goin' away from here.

WILETTA: Shoulda gone 'fore you started this misery.

(Manners indicates that she should get rougher; she tries.)

Screamin' 'bout your rights! You got none! You got none!

JOHN: I'm askin' for help, I gotta leave.

MANNERS *(To John)*: Appeal, remember it's an appeal.

JOHN *(As though a light has dawned)*: Ah, you're so right. *(Reads with tender appeal)* I gotta leave.

MANNERS: Right.

WILETTA: You tryin' to tell me that you runnin' away?

SHELDON *(Worried about Job's escape and getting caught up outside of the scene)*: Sure! That's what he said in the line right there!

(Manners silences Sheldon with a gesture.)

WILETTA: You say you ain't done nothin' wrong?

(Manners looks at Eddie and Bill with despair.)

JOHN: I ain't lyin' . . .

WILETTA: Then there's no need to be runnin'. Ain't you got no faith?

SHELDON *(Sings in a shaky voice as he raps out time)*:
Oh, well, a time of trouble is a lonesome time
Time of trouble is a lonesome time . . .

(Joined by Millie:)

Feel like I could die, feel like I could die . . .

WILETTA: Tell 'em you sorry, tell 'em you done wrong!

MANNERS: Relate, Wiletta. Relate to what's going on around you! *(To John)* Go on.

JOHN: I wasn't even votin' for a Black man, votin' for somebody white same as they. *(Aside to Manners)* Too much? Too little? I fell off.

(Manners indicates that he's on the beam.)

WILETTA: I ain't never voted!

SHELDON: No, Lord!

WILETTA: I don't care who get in! Don't make no nevermind to us!

MILLIE: The truth?

JOHN *(All afire)*: When a man got a decent word to say for us down here, I gonna vote for him.

WILETTA: A decent word! And that's all you ever gonna get outta him. Damnit! He ain't gonna win no how! They done said he ain't and they gonna see to it! And you gonna be dead . . . for a decent word!

JOHN: I ain't gonna wait to be killed.

WILETTA: There's only one right thing to do!

(Cast turns page in unison.)

You got to go and give yourself up.

JOHN: But I ain't done nothin'.

SHELDON *(Starts to sing again)*: Wella, trouble is a lonesome thing . . . lonesome . . . lonesome . . .

MANNERS *(The song even grates on him)*: Cut it, it's too much.

JUDY: My father will have you put in the county jail where you'll be safe.

JOHN: But I ain't done nothin'!

JUDY: I'm thinking of Ruby and the others, even if you aren't. I don't want murder in this community.

WILETTA *(Screams)*: Boy, get down on your knees.

MANNERS *(To Eddie)*: Muscular tension.

(Eddie makes a note.)

WILETTA: Oh, Lord, touch this boy's heart!

SHELDON: Mmmmmm, hmmmmmmmmmm. Hmmmmmmm . . .

WILETTA: Reach him tonight! Take the fear and hatred out of his soul!

MILLIE: Mercy, Lord!

JOHN: Stop, I can't stand no more. Whatever you say, anything you say.

SHELDON: Praise the Lord!

EDDIE: Renard enters.

BILL: Carrie, you shouldn't be here.

WILETTA: I told her. I'm beggin' you to help my boy, sir . . .

(She drops script and picks it up.)

JOHN: Ohhh, I can't sustain.

MANNERS: Don't try. We're breaking everything down to the simplest components . . . I want simple reactions to given circumstances in order to highlight the outstanding phases.

(Wiletta finds her place.)

Okay, let it roll.

WILETTA: I'm beggin' you to help my boy.

BILL: Boy, you're a mighty little fella to fly in the face of things people live by 'round here. I'll do what I can, what little I can.

WILETTA: Thank you, sir.

JUDY: Have Judge Willis put him in jail where he'll be safe.

BILL: Guess it wasn't his fault.

WILETTA: He don' know nothin'.

BILL: There are all kinds of white men in the world.

SHELDON: The truth.

BILL: This bird Akins got to sayin' the kind of things that was bound to stir you folks up.

MILLIE: I ain't paid him no mind myself.

BILL: Well, anything you want to take to the jailhouse with you? Like a washcloth and . . . well, whatever you might need.

JOHN: I don't know, don't know what I'm doin'.

BILL: Think you learned a lesson from all this?

MILLIE: You hear Mr. Renard?

SHELDON: He wanna know if you learned your lesson.

JOHN: I believed I was right.

SHELDON: Now you know you wasn't.

BILL: If anything happens, you tell the men Mr. Akins put notions in your head, understand?

SHELDON: He wanna know if you understand.

BILL: Come along, we'll put you in the jailhouse. Reckon I owe your ma and pa that much.

JOHN: I'm afraid, I so afraid . . .

MILLIE: Just go, 'fore they get here.

EDDIE: Job turns and looks at his father.

(Sheldon places one finger to his lips and throws up his arms to show that he has no line.)

Finally, he looks to his mother, she goes back to her ironing.

BILL: Petunia, see that Miss Carrie gets home safe.

MILLIE: Yes, sir.

EDDIE: Job follows Renard out into the night as Ruby starts to sing.

WILETTA *(Sings)*:
> Keep me from sinkin' down
> O, Lord, O, my Lord
> Keep me from sinkin' down . . .

MANNERS: Cut, relax, at ease!

MILLIE *(Brushes lint from her skirt)*: I'll have to bring work clothes.

SHELDON *(To Millie)*: I almost hit the number yesterday.

MILLIE: I'm glad you didn't.

(Bill crosses to Manners; we hear snatches of their conversation as the others cross-talk.)

JUDY *(To John)*: Did you finish my book?

(John claps his hand to his forehead in a typical Manners gesture.)

BILL *(A light conference on Wiletta)*: A line of physical action might . . .

SHELDON *(To Millie)*: I almost got an apartment.

MANNERS: Limited emotional capacity.

MILLIE *(To Sheldon)*: *Almost* doesn't mean a thing.

MANNERS: Well, it's coming. Sheldon, I like what's happening.

SHELDON: Thank you, does he give himself up to Judge Willis and get saved?

MANNERS *(Flabbergasted, as are John, Judy, Bill and Eddie)*: Shel, haven't you read it? Haven't you heard us read it?

SHELDON: No, I just go over and over my own lines, I ain't in the last of the third act.

JUDY: Are my motivations coming through?

MANNERS: Yeah, forget it. Sit down, Sheldon . . . just for you . . . Renard drives him toward jail, deputies stop them on the way, someone shoots and kills Job as he tries to escape, afterward they find out he was innocent, Renard makes everyone feel like a dog . . . they realize they were wrong and so forth.

SHELDON: And so forth.

MANNERS: He makes them realize that lynching is wrong.

(He refers to his notes.)

SHELDON *(To Wiletta)*: What was he innocent of?

WILETTA: I don't know.

JOHN: About the voting.

SHELDON: Uh-uh, he was guilty of that 'cause he done confessed.

MANNERS: Innocent of wrongdoing, Sheldon.

SHELDON: Uh-huh, oh, yeah.

MANNERS: Yale, you're on the right track. John, what can I say? You're great. Millie, you're growing, gaining command . . . I begin to feel an inner as well as the outer rendering.

JOHN: If we could run the sequence without interruption.

SHELDON: Yeah, then we would motorate and all that.

MANNERS *(To Wiletta)*: Dear heart, I've got to tell you . . .

WILETTA: I ain't so hot.

MANNERS: Don't be sensitive, let me help you, will you?

WILETTA *(Trying to handle Manners in the same way as John and Judy)*: I know my relations and motivations may not be just so . . .

SHELDON *(Wisely)*: Uh-huh, *motivation*, that's the thing.

WILETTA: They not right and I think I know why . . .

MANNERS: Darling, that's my department, will you listen?

(John is self-conscious about Wiletta and Sheldon. He is ashamed of them and has reached the point where he exchanges knowing looks with Bill, Eddie and Manners.)

WILETTA: You don't ever listen to me. You hear the others but not me. And it's 'cause of the school. 'Cause they know 'bout justifyin' and the antagonist . . . I never studied that, so you don't want to hear me, that's all right.

JUDY *(Stricken to the heart)*: Oh, don't say that.

SHELDON: He listen to me, and I ain't had it.

JOHN *(Starts to put his arm around Wiletta)*: Oh, Wiletta . . .

WILETTA *(Moving away from him)*: Oh, go on.

MANNERS: Wiletta, dear, I'm sorry if I've complicated things. I'll make it as clear as I can. You are pretending to act and I can see through your pretense. I want truth. What is truth? Truth is simply whatever you can bring yourself to believe, that is all. You must have integrity about your work . . . a sense of . . . well, sense.

WILETTA: I'm tryin' to lose myself like you say but . . .

JOHN *(Wants to help but afraid to interrupt)*: Oh, no . . .

MANNERS *(Sternly)*: You can't lose yourself, you are you . . . and you can't get away. You, Wiletta, must relate.

SHELDON: That's what I do.

WILETTA: I don't see why the boy couldn't get away . . . it's the killin' that . . . something's wrong. I may be in fast company but I got as much integrity as any. I didn't start workin' no yesterday.

MANNERS: No, Wiletta, no self-pity. Look, he can't escape this death. We want audience sympathy. We have a very subtle point to make, very subtle . . .

BILL: I hate the kind of play that bangs you over the head with the message. Keep it subtle.

MANNERS *(Getting very basic)*: We don't want to antagonize the audience.

WILETTA: It'll make 'em mad if he gets away?

MANNERS: This is a simple, sweet, lovable guy. Sheldon, does it offend you that he gives himself up to Judge Willis?

SHELDON: No, not if that's how they do.

MANNERS: We're making one beautiful, clear point . . . violence is wrong.

WILETTA: My friend, Miss Green, say she don't see why they act like this.

(John thinks he knows how to handle Wiletta. He is about to burst with an idea. Manners decides to let John wade in.)

JOHN: Look, think of the intellectual level here . . . they're underprivileged, uneducated . . .

WILETTA *(Letting John know he's treading on thin ice)*: Look out, you ain't so smart.

JOHN *(Showing so much of Manners)*: They've probably never seen a movie or television . . . never used a telephone. They . . . they're not like us. They're good, kind, folksy people . . . but they're ignorant, they just don't know.

WILETTA: You ain't the director.

SHELDON *(To John)*: You better hush.

MANNERS: We're dealing with simple, backward people but they're human beings.

WILETTA: 'Cause they colored, you tellin' me they're human bein's . . . I *know* I'm a human bein' . . . Listen here . . .

MANNERS: I will not listen! It does not matter to me that they're Negroes. Black, white, green, or purple, I maintain there is only one race . . . the human race.

(Sheldon bursts into applause.)

MILLIE: That's true.

MANNERS: Don't think "Negro," think "people."

SHELDON: Let's stop segregatin' ourselves.

JOHN *(To Wiletta)*: I didn't mean any harm, you don't understand . . .

BILL *(To Millie as he looks heavenward and acts out his weariness)*: Oh, honey child!

MILLIE: Don't call me no damn honey child!

BILL: Well, is my face red?

MILLIE: Yeah, and on you it looks good.

MANNERS: What's going on?

MILLIE: Honey child.

WILETTA *(Mumbling as all dialogue falls pell-mell)*: Justify.

BILL *(With great resignation)*: Trying to be friendly.

WILETTA: Justify.

MILLIE: Get friendly with someone else.

MANNERS: May we have order!

SHELDON *(In a terrible flash of temper)*: That's why they don't do more colored shows! Always fightin'! Everybody hush, let this man direct! He don't even have to be here! Right now he could be out in Hollywood in the middle of a big investigation!

EDDIE: The word is production!

SHELDON: That's what I said, production.

EDDIE: No, you didn't.

SHELDON: What'd I say?

MANNERS *(Bangs table)*: I will not countenance another outbreak of this nature. I say to each and every one of you . . . I am in charge and I'll thank you to remember it. I've been much too lax, too informal. Well, it doesn't work. There's going to be order.

WILETTA: I was only sayin' . . .

MANNERS: I said *everyone*! My patience is at an end. I demand your concentrated attention. It's as simple as A, B, C, if you will apply yourselves. The threat of this horrible violence throws you into cold, stark fear. It's a perfectly human emotion, anyone would feel it. I'm not asking you to dream up some fantastic horror . . . it's a lynching. We've never actually seen such a thing, thank God . . . but allow your imagination to soar, to take hold of it . . . think.

SHELDON: I seen one.

MANNERS *(Can't believe he heard right)*: What?

BILL: What did you see?

SHELDON: A lynchin', when I was a little boy 'bout nine years old.

JUDY: Oh, no.

WILETTA: How did it happen? Tell me, Sheldon, did you really?

MANNERS: Would it help you to know, Wiletta?

WILETTA: I . . . guess . . . I don't know.

BILL *(Not eager to hear about it)*: Will it bother you, Sheldon? It could be wrong for him . . . I don't know . . .

(Eddie gives Manners a doubtful look.)

MILLIE: That must be something to see.

MANNERS *(With a sigh)*: Go on, Sheldon.

(Manners watches cast reactions.)

SHELDON: I think it was on a Saturday, yeah, it had to be or else-wise I woulda been in the field with my ma and pa.

WILETTA: What field?

SHELDON: The cotton field. My ma said I was too little to go every day, but some of 'em younger'n me was out there all the time. My grandma was home with me . . .

(Sheldon thinks of his grandma and almost forgets his story.)

WILETTA: What about the lynchin'?

SHELDON: It was Saturday and rainin' a sort of sifty rain. I was standin' at the window watchin' the lilac bush wavin' in the wind. A sound come to my ears like bees hummin' . . . was voices comin' closer and closer, screamin' and cursin'. My granny tried to pull me from the window. "Come on, chile," she said, "they gonna kill us all . . . hide!" But I was fightin' to keep from goin' with her, scared to go in the dark closet.

(Judy places her hands over her ears and bows her head.)

The screamin' comin' closer and closer . . . and the screamin' was laughin' . . . Lord, how they was laughin' . . . louder and louder.

(Sheldon rises and puts in his best performance to date. He raises one hand and creates a stillness . . . everyone is spellbound.)

Hush! Then I hear wagon wheels bumpin' over the wet, stony road, chains clankin'. Man drivin' the wagon, beatin' the horse . . . Ahhhhhhhh! Ahhhhhhhh! Horse just pullin' along . . . and then I saw it! Chained to the back of the wagon, draggin' and bumpin' along . . .

(He opens his arms wide.)

The arms of it stretched out . . . a burnt, naked thing . . . a burnt, naked thing that once was a man . . . and I started to scream but no sound come out . . . just a screamin' but no sound . . .

(He lowers his arms and brings the company back to the present.)

That was Mr. Morris that they killed. Mr. Morris. I remember one time he come to our house and was laughin' and talkin' about everything . . . and he give us a fruitcake that his wife made. Folks said he was crazy . . . you know, 'bout talkin' back . . . quick to speak his mind. I left there when I was seventeen. I don't want to live in no place like that.

MANNERS: When I hear of barbarism . . . I feel so wretched, so guilty.

SHELDON: Don't feel that way. You wouldn't kill nobody and do 'em like that . . . would you?

MANNERS *(Hurt by the question)*: No, Sheldon.

SHELDON: That's what I know.

(Bill crosses and rests his hand on Sheldon's shoulder. Sheldon flinches because he hadn't noticed Bill's approach.)

Oh! I didn't see you. Did I help y'all by tellin' that story?

MANNERS: It was quite an experience. I'm shot. Break for lunch, we'll pick up in an hour, have a good afternoon session.

MILLIE: Makes me feel like goin' out in the street and crackin' heads.

JUDY *(Shocked)*: Oh!

EDDIE: Makes my blood boil . . . but what can you do?

MANNERS: We're doing a play.

MILLIE *(To Judy)*: I'm starved. You promised to show us that Italian place.

JUDY *(Surprised that Millie no longer feels violent)*: Why . . . sure, I'd love to. Let's have a festive lunch, with wine!

SHELDON: Yeah, that wine that comes in a straw bottle.

JUDY: Imported wine.

MILLIE: And chicken cacciatore . . . let's live!

(Wiletta crosses to Manners while others are getting coats; she has hit on a scheme to make Manners see her point.)

WILETTA: Look here, I ain't gonna let you get mad with me. You supposed to be my buddy.

JOHN: Let's go!

(Manners opens his arms to Wiletta.)

MANNERS: I'm glad you said that. You're my sweetheart.

MILLIE: Bill, how about you?

BILL *(Places his hand on his stomach)*: The Italian place. Okay, count me in.

EDDIE *(Stacking scripts)*: I want a king-size dish of clams . . . raw ones.

WILETTA: Wouldn't it be nice if the mother could say, "Son, you right! I don't want to send you outta here but I don't know what to do . . ."

MANNERS: Darling, darling . . . no.

MILLIE: Wiletta, get a move on.

WILETTA: Or else she says, "Run for it, Job!" and then they catch him like that . . . he's dead *anyway*, see?

MANNERS *(Trying to cover his annoyance)*: It's not the script, it's *you*. Bronson does the writing, you do the acting, it's that simple.

SHELDON: One race, the human race. I like that.

JUDY: Veal parmesan with oodles and oodles of cheese!

WILETTA: I was just thinkin' if I could . . .

MANNERS *(Indicating script)*: Address yourself to this.

JUDY *(To John)*: Bring my book tomorrow.

JOHN: Cross my heart.

WILETTA: I just wanted to talk about . . .

MANNERS: You are going to get a spanking.

(He leaves with Eddie and others.)

MILLIE: Wiletta, come on!

WILETTA *(Abruptly)*: I . . . I'll be there later.

MILLIE *(Miffed by the short answer)*: Suit yourself.

JUDY *(To Wiletta)*: It's on the corner of Sixth Avenue on this side of the street.

JOHN: Correction. Correction, Avenue of the Americas.

ALICE CHILDRESS

(Laughter from Manners, Millie, Sheldon and Bill offstage.)

JUDY *(Posturing in her best theatrical style)*: But no one, absolutely no one ever says it. He's impossible, absolutely impossible!
WILETTA: Oh, ain't he though.

(John bows to Judy and indicates that she goes first.)

JOHN: Dear Gaston, Alphonse will follow.
WILETTA: John, I told you everything wrong 'cause I didn't know better, that's the size of it. No fool like an old fool. You right, don't make sense to be bowin' and scrapin' and Tommin' . . . No, don't pay no attention to what I said.
JOHN *(Completely Manners)*: Wiletta, my dear, you're my sweet-heart, I love you madly and I think you're wonderfully magnificent!

(Judy suddenly notices his posturing and hers; she feels silly. She laughs, laughter bordering on tears.)

JUDY: John, you're a puppet with strings attached and so am I. Everyone's a stranger and I'm the strangest of all.

(She quickly leaves.)

JOHN: Wiletta, don't forget to come over!

(He follows Judy.)

WILETTA *(Paces up and down, tries doing her lines aloud)*: Only one thing to do, give yourself up! Give yourself up . . . give up . . . give up . . . give up . . . give up . . . give up.

(Lights whirl and flicker. Blues record comes in loud, then down, lights flicker to indicate passage of time. Wiletta is gone. Stage is empty.

Bill enters, removing his coat. He has a slight attack of indigestion and belches his disapproval of pizza pie. Others can be heard laughing and talking offstage.)

BILL: Ohhhhhh, ahhhhh . . .

(Manners enters with Eddie. Eddie proceeds to the table and script. Manners is just getting over the effects of a good laugh . . . but his mirth suddenly fades as he crosses to Bill.)

MANNERS: I am sorry you felt compelled to tell that joke about the colored minister and the stolen chicken.

BILL: Trying to be friendly . . . I don't know . . . I even ate pizza.

EDDIE: I always *think* . . . think first, is this the right thing to say, would I want anyone to say this to me?

(Burst of laughter from offstage.)

BILL: Oh, you're so noble, you give me a pain in the ass. Love thy neighbor as thyself, now I ask you, is that a reasonable request?

MANNERS *(For fear the others will hear)*: All right. Knock it off.

BILL: Okay, I said I was sorry, but for what . . . I'll never know.

(Sheldon, Millie, Judy and John enter in a hilarious mood. Judy is definitely feeling the wine. Sheldon is supplying the fun.)

SHELDON: Sure, I was workin' my hind parts off . . . Superintendent of the buildin' . . .

JOHN: But the tenants, Shel! That's a riot!

SHELDON: One day a man came along and offered me fifty dollars a week just to walk across the stage real slow. *(Mimics his acting role)* Sure, I took it! Hard as I worked I was glad to slow down!

(Others laugh.)

JUDY *(Holds her head)*: Ohhhhhh, that wine.

MILLIE: Wasn't it good? I wanna get a whole *case* of it for the holidays. All that I have to do! My liquors, wreathes, presents, cards . . . I'm gonna buy my husband a tape recorder.

JUDY *(To John)*: I'm sorry I hurt your feelings but you are a little puppet, and I'm a little puppet, and all the world . . .

(She impresses the lesson by tapping John on his chest.)

MANNERS: Judy, I want to go over something with you . . .

JUDY: No, you don't . . . you're afraid I'm going to . . . hic. 'Fraid I'll go overboard on the friendship deal and *com*plicate matters . . . complications . . .

MANNERS: Two or three glasses of wine, she's delirious. Do you want some black coffee?

JUDY: No, no, I only have hiccups.

MILLIE *(To John)*: Which would you rather have, a tape recorder or a camera?

JOHN: I don't know.

SHELDON: I'd rather have some money, make mine cash.

MANNERS *(To Judy)*: Why don't you sit down and get yourself together?

(She sits.)

JOHN *(To Manners)*: I . . . I think I have some questions about Wiletta and the third act.

MANNERS: It's settled, don't worry, John, she's got it straight.

JOHN: I know but it seems . . .

MANNERS: Hoskins sat out front yesterday afternoon. He's mad about you. First thing he says, "Somebody's going to try and steal that boy from us."

JOHN *(Very pleased)*: I'm glad I didn't know he was there.

MANNERS: Eddie, call it, will you? Okay, attention!

EDDIE: Beginning of the third.

(Company quiets down, opens scripts. Wiletta enters.)

MANNERS: You're late.

WILETTA: I know it. *(To Millie)* I had a bowl of soup and was able to relate to it and justify, no trouble at all. *(To Manners)* I'm not gonna take up your time now but I wanta see you at the end of the afternoon.

MANNERS: Well . . . I . . . I'll let you know . . . we'll see.

WILETTA: It's important.

MANNERS *(Ignoring her and addressing entire company)*: Attention, I want to touch on a corner of what we did this morning and then we'll highlight the rest of three!

(Actors rise and start for places.)

John, top of page four.

JOHN: When a man has a decent word to say for us down here, I gonna vote for him.

WILETTA *(With real force; she is lecturing him rather than scolding)*: A decent word? And that's all you ever gonna get out of him. Damnit, he ain't gonna win no how. They done said he ain't and they gonna see to it! And you gonna be dead for a decent word.

MANNERS *(To Eddie)*: This is deliberate.

JOHN: I gotta go, I ain't gonna wait to be killed.

WILETTA: There's only one right thing to do. You got to go and give yourself up.

JOHN: I ain't done nothin'.

JUDY: My father will have Judge Willis put you in the county jail where you'll be safe.

(Manners is quite disheartened.)

WILETTA: Job, she's tryin' to help us.

JUDY: I'm thinking of the others even if you aren't. I don't want murder in this community.

WILETTA: Boy, get down on your knees.

(John falls to his knees.)

Oh, Lord touch this boy's heart. Reach him tonight, take the fear and hatred out of his soul!

SHELDON: Hmmmmmmm, mmmmmmmm, mmmmmmmmm . . .

MILLIE: Mercy, Lord.

JOHN: Stop, I can't stand anymore . . .

(Wiletta tries to raise John.)

MANNERS: No, keep him on his knees.

JOHN: I can't stand anymore . . . whatever you say . . .

(Again Wiletta tries to raise him.)

SHELDON *(To Wiletta)*: He say keep him on his knees.

WILETTA: Aw, get up off the floor, wallowin' around like that.

(Everyone is shocked.)

MANNERS: Wiletta, this is not the time or place to . . .

WILETTA: All that crawlin' and goin' on before me . . . hell, I ain't the one tryin' to lynch him. This ain't sayin' nothin', don't make sense. Talkin' 'bout the truth is anything I can believe . . . well, I don't believe this.

MANNERS: I will not allow you to interrupt in this disorganized manner.

WILETTA: You been askin' me what I think and where things come from and how come I thought it and all that. Where is this comin' from?

(Company murmuring in the background.)

Tell me, why this boy's people turned against him? Why we sendin' him out into the teeth of a lynch mob? I'm his mother and I'm sendin' him to his death. This is a lie.

JOHN: But his mother doesn't understand . . . There have been cases of men dragged from their homes . . .

WILETTA: But they was *dragged* . . . they come with guns and dragged 'em out. They weren't sent to be killed by their mama. The writer wants the damn white man to be the hero—and me the villain.

MILLIE: I think we're all tired.

SHELDON: Outta order, outta order, you outta order. This ain't the time.

MANNERS: Wiletta, there are some who may deserve this from you but I'm not the one.

SHELDON: No, you ain't.

MANNERS: As long as I've known you, you've never given me any trouble.

WILETTA: And that's what's the matter.

MANNERS: What do you want to do when the mob comes after Job? Shoot it out? That's sheer violence.

WILETTA: Yeah, kill my child and call me violent, that's what comes of all the justifyin'.

MANNERS: I'm going to tell you something you've never known before now. Remember the last picture we made together? You played a character part. I had to sweat blood, stayed up all night with the writers . . . getting them to change a stereotype mammy role into something decent for you . . .

WILETTA: And when you got through, damnit, it was still a mammy part. Character part! Lemme tell you 'bout them character parts.

(She startles company by falling into character) "Oh, Miss Wentworth, I'm so distress, I don't know what to do."

(Falls out of character) Always distressed and don't know a damn thing to do!

(Back into character) "It's 'bout my son, he's a good boy but he's got notions that's gonna get him in trouble."

(Out of character) Our sons always got notions that they as good as anybody else, and we always askin' the white folks we work for to change their minds for 'em! We got husbands too, you may not see 'em but you hear 'bout 'em in those character parts.

(In character) "I don't know why I stays with that man, he won't work, he won't come home, I don't know why I loves him, guess it's 'cause he keeps me laughin' all the time."

(Out of character) You ever hear of a lazy, no-good, two-timin' man keepin' a woman laughin' all the time? Character part!

A baby in my arms. *(In character)* "You're my little angel, and just like I raised your mama, I'm gonna raise you to be a little lady."

(Making up her own act) Dear little baby of the folks I work for, I got a present for you . . . my whole damn life! I'm handin' it over to you and your ma and pa. If you got no money to pay me, I wanna stay anyhow, my pleasure is to wait on you forever. To hell with my children and hooray for you!

(Out of character) You stayin' up all night fixin' up character parts for me! Givin' 'em what you call dignity! Dignity! You know what your dignity is? A old black straw hat with a flower stickin' up in front, hands folded 'cross my stomach, sayin' the same damn fool things . . . only nice and easy and proper!

(In character) "I know it's none of my business, Mrs. Sanders, but I just got to say it. You haven't been yourself lately and it grieves me to see you eatin' your heart out

'bout Mr. John. I try to pretend I don't see it, but I do. It's almost more than a body can stand."

MANNERS: I'm sorry you've had to play maids but it's not my fault . . .

WILETTA: They're not maids. What you call maids aren't even people! I got news for you. We don't give a damn 'bout Mr. John or Mr. Renard either. I don't sit down and eat with 'em and I ain't sittin' up nights worryin' 'bout 'em. Dignity! All them lyin' pictures I seen with white folks pretendin' they passin' for white? When they wanta show a colored girl passin', they go and get this child to do it. *(Points to Judy)*

MILLIE: Exactly.

WILETTA: Who gets to play the Indian Chief? Look close and you'll see he's got blue eyes, and you gonna tell me 'bout truth and justifyin'? And don't dare be BLACK . . . then you got to scratch your head *(Demonstrates)* every time you start to think . . . plowin' up thoughts. Justify! Oh, I'm holdin' class today.

BILL: Wiletta, I've had to do roles that I found objectionable.

WILETTA: I'm wise. But you don't give a damn 'cause a lynch mob ain't after you! I know what you play . . . turnin' into a fanged wolf when the moon is full, turnin' into a vampire bat, a blood-sucker! You *had* to go to school to justify that. On that tee-vee box y'all shootin' down each other every night, all night long. Shootin' and kissin', that's all you know . . . how big is your bust and murder, murder, murder. Yes indeed, that's *your* stereotype. Suit yourself, but I'm sicka mine. I'm full, my cup runneth over. *(Points to script)* Would you . . . could you do this to a son of yours?

MANNERS: She places him in the hands of Judge Willis and . . .

WILETTA: And I tell you she knows better.

BILL: It's only because she trusts and believes. Couldn't you trust and believe in Al?

MANNERS: Bill, please.

WILETTA: No, I wouldn't trust him with my son's life.

MANNERS: Thank you.

SHELDON: She don't mean it.

WILETTA: Judge Willis! Why don't his people help him?

MANNERS: The story goes a certain way and . . .

WILETTA: It oughta go another way.

ENTIRE COMPANY (*In unison*): Talk about it later. We're all tired. Yes. We need a rest. Sometimes your own won't help you.

MANNERS: Leave her alone!

(Manners is on fire now. He loves the challenge of this conflict and is determined to win the battle. He must win.)

Why this great fear of death? Christ died for something and . . .

WILETTA: Sure, they came and got him and hauled him off to jail. His mother didn't turn him in, in fact, the one who did it was one of them so-called friends.

MANNERS: His death proved something. Job's death brings him the lesson.

WILETTA: That they should stop lynchin' *innocent* men! Fine thing! Lynch the guilty, is that the idea? The dark-skinned Oliver Twist. *(Points to John)* That's you. Yeah, I mean, you got to go to school to justify this!

MANNERS: Wiletta, I've listened. I've heard you out . . .

WILETTA (*To Sheldon*): And you echoin' every damn word he says—"Keep him on his knees."

MANNERS: I've heard you out and even though you think you know more than the author . . .

WILETTA: You don't want to hear. You are a prejudiced man, a prejudiced racist.

(Gasp from company.)

MANNERS (*Caught off guard*): I will not accept that from you or anyone else.

WILETTA: I told this boy to laugh and grin at everything you said, well . . . I ain't laughin'.

MANNERS: While you give me hell-up-the-river, I'm supposed to stand here and take it with a tolerance beyond human endurance. I'm white! You think it's so wonderful to be white? I've got troubles up to here! But I don't expect anyone to hand me anything and it's high time you got rid of that notion. No, I never worked in a cotton field. I didn't. I was raised in a nice, comfortable, nine-room house in the Midwest . . . and I learned to say nigger, kike, sheeny, spick, dago, wop, and chink . . . I hear 'em plenty! I was raised by a sweet, dear, kind old aunt, who spent her time gathering funds for missionaries . . . but she almost turned our town upside down when Mexicans moved in on our block. I know about troubles . . . my own! I've never been *handed* any gifts. Oh, it's so grand to be white! I had to crawl and knuckle under step by step. What I want and what I believe, indeed! I directed blood, guts, fistfights, bedroom farces, and the lowest kind of dirtied-up sex until I earned the respect of this business.

WILETTA: But would you send your son out to . . .

MANNERS: I proclaim this National Truth Week! Whites! You think we belong to one great, grand fraternity? They stole and snatched from me for years, and I'm a club member! Ever hear of an idea man? They picked my brains! They stripped me! They threw me cash and I let the credit go! My brains milked, while somebody else climbed on my back to take bows. But I didn't beg for mercy . . . why waste your breath? I learned one thing that's the only damned truth worth knowing . . . you get nothin' for nothin', but nothin'! No favors, no dreams served up on silver platters. Now . . . finally I get something for all of us . . . but it's not enough for you! I'm prejudiced! Get wise, there's damned few of us interested in putting on a colored show at all, much less one that's going to say anything. It's rough out here, it's a hard world! Do you think I can stick my neck out by telling the truth about you? There are billions of things that *can't be said* . . . do you follow me, billions! Where the hell do you think I can raise a hundred thousand dollars to tell the unvarnished truth?

(Picks up the script and waves it.)

So, maybe it's a lie . . . but it's one of the finest lies you'll come across for a damned long time! Here's bitter news, since you're livin' off truth . . . The American public is not ready to see you the way you want to be seen because, one, they don't believe it, two, they don't want to believe it, and three, they're convinced they're superior—and that, my friend, is why Carrie and Renard have to carry the ball! Get it? Now you wise up and aim for the soft spot in that American heart, let 'em pity you, make 'em weep buckets, be helpless, make 'em feel so damned sorry for you that they'll lend a hand in easing up the pressure. You've got a free ride. Coast, baby, coast.

WILETTA: Would you send your son out to be murdered?

MANNERS *(So wound up, he answers without thinking)*: Don't compare yourself to me! What goes for my son doesn't necessarily go for yours! Don't compare him *(Points to John)* . . . with three strikes against him, don't compare him with my son, they've got nothing in common . . . not a goddamn thing!

(He realizes what he has said, also that he has lost company sympathy. He is utterly confused and embarrassed by his own statement.)

I tried to make it clear.

JOHN: It is clear.

(Manners quickly exits to dressing room. Eddie follows him. Judy has an impulse to follow.)

BILL: No, leave him alone.

JOHN *(To Wiletta)*: I feel like a fool . . . Hmmph. "Don't think Negro, think *people*."

SHELDON *(To Bill)*: You think he means we're fired?

BILL: I don't know . . . I don't know . . .

MILLIE: Wiletta, this should have been discussed with everyone first.

SHELDON: Done talked yourself out of a job.

BILL: Shel, you don't know that.

(During the following scene, Sheldon is more active and dynamic than ever before.)

SHELDON: Well, he didn't go out there to bake her no birthday cake.

(Judy is quietly crying.)

MILLIE: We got all the truth we bargained for and then some.

WILETTA: Yes, I spoke my mind and he spoke his.

BILL: We have a company representative, Sheldon is the deputy. Any complaints we have should be handled in an orderly manner. Equity has rules, the rule book says . . .

SHELDON: I left my rule book home. Furthermore, I don't think I want to be the deputy.

MILLIE: He was dead right about some things but I didn't appreciate that *last* remark.

SHELDON *(To Wiletta)*: You can't spit in somebody's eye and tell 'em you was washin' it out.

BILL: Sheldon, now is not the time to resign.

SHELDON (*Taking charge*): All right, I'm tryin' to lead 'em, tryin'
to play peacemaker. Shame on y'all! Look at the U.N.!

MILLIE: The U.N.?

SHELDON: Yes, the United Nations. You think they run their
business by blabbin' everything they think? No! They talk
sweet and polite 'til they can outslick the next feller. Wisdom!
The greatest gift in the world, they got it! (*To Wiletta*) Way
you talked, I thought you had the 'tomic bomb.

WILETTA: I'm sick of people signifyin' we got no sense.

SHELDON: I know. I'm the only man in the house and what am
I doin'? Whittlin' a doggone stick. But I whittled it, didn't
I? I can't write a play and I got no money to put one on . . .
Yes! I'm gonna whittle my stick!

(*Stamps his foot to emphasize the point.*)

JOHN (*Very noble and very worried*): How do you go about putting
in a notice?

SHELDON (*To John*): Hold on 'til I get to you. (*To Wiletta*) Now,
when he gets back here, you be sure and tell him.

WILETTA: Tell him what?

SHELDON: Damn, tell him you *sorry*.

BILL: Oh, he doesn't want that.

WILETTA: Shame on him if he does.

MILLIE: I don't want to spend the rest of the day wondering why
he walked out.

WILETTA: I'm playin' a leadin' part and I want this script changed
or else.

SHELDON: Hush up, before the man hears you.

MILLIE: Just make sure you're not the one to tell him. You're a
great one for runnin' to management and telling your guts.

SHELDON: I never told management nothin', anybody say I did
is lyin'.

JUDY: Let's ask for a *quiet* talk to straighten things out.

BILL: No. This is between Wiletta and Manners and I'm sure they can . . .

JOHN: We all ought to show some integrity.

SHELDON: Integrity . . . got us in a big mess.

MILLIE *(To John)*: You can't put in your notice until after opening night. You've got to follow Equity rules . . .

SHELDON: Yeah, he's trying to defy the union.

WILETTA *(Thumping the script)*: This is a damn lie.

MILLIE: But you can't tell people what to write, that's censorship.

SHELDON *(To Wiletta)*: And that's another point in your disfavor.

JOHN: They can write what they want but we don't have to do it.

SHELDON: You outta order!

BILL *(To John)*: Oh, don't keep stirring it up, heaping on coals . . .

JUDY: Wiletta, maybe if we appeal to Mr. Hoskins or Mr. Bronson . . .

SHELDON: The producer and the author ain't gonna listen to her, after all . . . they white same as Manners.

JUDY: I resent that!

BILL: I do too, Shel.

JUDY: I've had an awful lot of digs thrown on me . . . remarks about white, white . . . and I do resent it.

JOHN *(To Judy)*: He means what can you expect from Sheldon. *(To Sheldon)* Sheldon.

BILL *(To Judy)*: I'm glad you said that.

SHELDON: I'm sorry, I won't say nothin' 'bout white. *(To Wiletta)* Look here, Hoskins, Manners, and Bronson . . . they got things in . . . er . . . common, you know what I mean?

WILETTA: Leave me alone . . . and suit yourselves.

MILLIE: I know what's right but I need this job.

SHELDON: There you go . . . talk.

WILETTA: Thought your husband doesn't want you to work.

MILLIE: He doesn't but I have to anyway.

JUDY: But you'll still be in New York. If this falls through I'll have to go back to Bridgeport . . . before I even get started.

JOHN: Maybe I'll never get another job.

MILLIE: Like Al Manners says, there's more to this life than the truth. *(To Judy)* You'll have to go to Bridgeport. Oh, how I wish I had a Bridgeport.

BILL: Okay, enough, *I'm* the villain. I get plenty of work, forgive me.

JUDY: Life scares me, honestly it does.

SHELDON: When you kick up a disturbance, the man's in his rights to call the cops . . . police car will come rollin' up here, next thing you know . . . you'll be servin' time.

MILLIE: Don't threaten her!

JOHN: Why don't you call a cop *for* him . . . try it.

(Henry enters carrying a paper bag.)

HENRY: I got Mr. Manners some nice danish, cheese, and prune.

MILLIE: He can't eat it right now . . . leave it there.

(Eddie enters with a shaken but stern attitude.)

EDDIE: Attention company. You are all dismissed for the day. I'll telephone about tomorrow's rehearsal.

SHELDON: Tell Mr. Manners I'm gonna memorize my first act.

(Eddie exits and Sheldon talks to company.)

I still owe the doctor money . . . and I can't lift no heavy boxes or be scrubbin' no floors. If I was a drinkin' man I'd get drunk.

MILLIE: Tomorrow is another day. Maybe everybody will be in better condition to . . . talk . . . just talk it all out. Let's go to the corner for coffee and a calm chat. *(Suddenly solicitous with Judy)* How about you, honey, wouldn't you like to relax and look over the situation? Bill?

BILL: I have to study for my soap opera . . . but thanks.

JUDY: Yes, let's go talk.

MILLIE: John? Wiletta, honey, let's go for coffee.

WILETTA: I'll be there after a while. Go on.

JOHN: We couldn't go without you.

SHELDON: We don't want to leave you by yourself in this old theater.

WILETTA: There are times when you got to be alone. *This is mine.*

(John indicates that they should leave. Millie, Sheldon, Judy, John and Bill exit.)

HENRY: Are you cryin'?

WILETTA: Yes.

HENRY: Ah, don't do that. It's too nice a day.

(Henry sits near tape recorder.)

I started to throw coffee at him that time when he kicked up a fuss, but you got to take a lotta things in this life.

WILETTA: Divide and conquer . . . that's the way they get the upper hand. A telephone call for tomorrow's rehearsal . . . they won't call me . . . But I'm gonna show up any damn way. The next move is his. He'll have to fire me.

HENRY: Whatcha say?

WILETTA: We have to go further and do better.

HENRY: That's a good one. I'll remember that. What's on this, music?

(Wiletta turns the machine on and down. The applause plays.)

WILETTA: Canned applause. When you need a bit of instant praise . . . you turn it on . . . and there you are.

(He tries it.)

HENRY: Canned applause. They got everything these days. Time flies. I bet you can't guess how old I am.

WILETTA: Not more than sixty.

HENRY: I'm seventy-eight.

WILETTA: Imagine that. A fine-lookin' man like you.

(Sound of police siren in street.)

HENRY: What's that?

WILETTA: Police siren.

HENRY: They got a fire engine house next to where I live. God-in-heaven, you never heard such a noise . . . and I'm kinda deaf . . . Didn't know that, did you?

WILETTA: No, I didn't. Some live by what they call great truths. Henry, I've always wanted to do somethin' real grand . . . in the theater . . . to stand forth at my best . . . to stand up here and do anything I want . . .

HENRY: Like my father . . . he was in vaudeville . . . doin' the soft-shoe and tippin' his hat to the ladies . . .

WILETTA: Yes, somethin' grand.

HENRY *(Adjusting the tape recorder to play applause)*: Do it . . . do it. I'm the audience.

WILETTA: I don't remember anything grand . . . I can't recall.

HENRY: Say somethin' from the Bible . . . like the twenty-third psalm.

WILETTA: Oh, I know.

(She comes downstage and recites beautifully from Psalm 133:)

> Behold how good and how pleasant it is for brethren to dwell together in unity. It is like the precious ointment upon the head, that ran down upon the beard, even Aaron's beard; that went down to the skirts of his garment; as the dew of Hermon, and

as the dew that descended upon the mountains of Zion; for there the Lord commanded the blessing, even life forevermore.

(Henry turns on applause as Wiletta stands tall for the curtain.)

END OF PLAY

STILL FOR A SECOND: AN AFTERWORD

Branden Jacobs-Jenkins

> Trouble in mind, I'm blue
> But I won't be blue always
> 'Cause the sun's gonna shine in my back door
>   some day

Trouble in Mind takes its title from a blues song first recorded in 1924 by vaudeville singer Thelma La Vizzo and its writer Richard M. Jones, but, like most standards, it would have been the subject of countless covers and reinterpretations by the time it found the playwright and actress Alice Childress. Bertha "Chippie" Hill popularized it on a 1926 recording with Louis Armstrong playing trumpet, and a decade later the genius of Georgia White would grace the annals of blues history with three different versions. Nina Simone has covered it, Aretha Franklin has covered it, Johnny Cash has covered it—each retooling the lyrics and instrumentation to fit their own style and spirit—but it is Dinah Washington's version that I like to imagine landing in our dramatist's ear, and which would have reached number four on the rhythm and blues charts right around the time the seeds of the playscript in your hands were likely beginning to take root in the author's mind.

This would have been around 1952, making this lyric a generation old and its concerns with an implicitly Black and female narrator discovering a new capacity for expression in the throes of psychological crisis that much closer to "perennial" status as an American theme. What Washington brought to the song was a sultry polish and an almost intellectual sophistication to the old, raw crisis and its lament, a kind of exquisite finish that seems in simpatico to me with Childress's own art, tortured but bright.

> Trouble in mind, that's true
> I've almost lost my mind
> Life ain't worth while living, feel like I could die

Wiletta Mayer, the middle-aged actress at the center of Childress's masterpiece and first full-length play, is found to be in just such a crisis and it is her journey through and not quite out of it that is ours to share. This is the story of a woman waking up in the middle of her life to the fact that the thing to which she's devoted a great part of her existence has been the source of its greatest despair. This thing has warped and deformed her very sense of self, let alone her dreams for it, leaving her stuck, embittered, alone, and betrayed.

That the thing in question turns out to be nothing more or less than the theater—its gifts misunderstood, perverted, and sullied in the hands of the wrong practitioners—is one of the play's central dramatic coups, pun intended. For Wiletta—and for us—the time has come to wrestle that self back from the vacuum of indifference, greed, cold cruelty, and self-delusion that emerges whenever an art form—or an industry—turns its back on the reality of human truth and suffering and that fight must take the form of the *doing* of the thing itself. And, in the process, Wiletta and her author manage to return to the art its own soul.

> *(Wiletta is suddenly moved by the sight of the theater. She holds up her hand for silence, looks out and up at the balcony. She loves the theater. She turns back to Henry.)*

WILETTA: A theater always makes me feel that way . . . gotta get still for a second.

You could miss it if you blinked—or, worse, mistake it for a "star entrance"—but this moment, this requisite stillness occurs just after the lights come up on the first act and it is the key to everything. To play this beat as simply an opportunity for the leading actor, however deserving, to stand onstage and soak up applause for merely being herself would be to not only undermine our heroine—whose hands are held up asking for *silence*—but to miss the play's opening argument. This is a story about a woman who, first and foremost, bears a love for the theater that is reverential. She is among its truest and humblest servants, the actor, and we are at the outset of something sacred. What Wiletta—and by extension Childress—is gesturing toward here is the redemptive holiness of the stage itself, the religiosity inherent in this act of communal imagining, why it must not be taken lightly and, most importantly, why it must be defended.

The theater is a spooky place and an even spookier practice. The actor's skill, in this art of illusion, is essentially alchemy, the reworking of her own flesh and breath so convincingly that onlookers begin to feel *as* and feel *for* a personage who, when the lights come up, is nowhere to be found. It is the place where reality can truly find itself not only suspended but transformed, where we are invited to see beyond our present into the future and the past, where phenomena such as haunting and possession approach the real, where the profane can truly don the trappings of the sacred and vice versa. It's radical, powerful, mind-altering stuff—and, as with anything dealing in the matters of the spirit made flesh, the stakes are always high. Hence its impressively ancient run as the storytelling form *du jour* for human societies trying to understand themselves. Hence the theater being, throughout history, one of the great objects of battle for commercial and political control.

And *Trouble in Mind* is about, among many things, control. A play within a play, it traces a war of the wills between the actors and director of *Chaos in Belleville*, a super cringey but definitely-believable-as-standard-fare-for-its-time Broadway-bound social drama by an absent white playwright which fumblingly depicts the lynching of a Black sharecropper's son who dares to vote. Aside from its tin-eared dialogue, desperate melodrama, and ridiculous depictions of just about everyone, the severest crime of *Chaos in Belleville* is actually that of self-importance. The director (aptly named Manners, as in those you are supposed to mind) and the other offstage powers-that-seem-to-be believe that, in addition to amassing ever more social and actual capital for themselves as creative professionals with this cockamamie play, they are also making "a contribution that really . . . leads to a clearer understanding." A contribution to whom and an understanding of what? That's never made clear to anyone. But, in the end, all Manners needs to reassure his company is a future in which they "draw pay envelopes for a long time to come." And that's that. As long as folks are getting paid, who cares why they're doing anything?

It is one of the great ironies of the piece that the egomaniacal Manners, high on his own supply of nobility, brings about his own foiling, demanding halfway through the first act that his actors—Black and white, male and female, young and old alike—"forget your old methods of work"—which is to say themselves—"and go along with me." His unorthodox ways quickly reveal themselves to be about manipulating and bullying people into a paralysis of self-consciousness—power games essentially, a patriarchy's greatest pastime. "Tension all over the place," one character remarks. And to what end? "The firm texture of truth," he pronounces after an awkward bout of actor torture.

Consequently, the intersectional ensemble of actors is thrown into and out of their own spirals, endlessly divided and redivided in their allegiances depending on their own shifting comforts with each other and the material and the grim real-life news of present-tense racial violence, which haunt the play's periphery. But, lucky for the viewer, it becomes Wiletta's fate to hold Manners's feet to the fire. "Truth."

> I'm gonna lay my head
> On some lonesome railroad line
> Let the 2:19 train ease my troubled mind

From a certain angle, this is a play about a certain kind of suicide—career suicide—and the actress who finally commits it and why, but, then again, suicide would imply that there was a life being lived in the lead-up to this grand act of self-immolation in the first place.

In fashioning Wiletta, Alice Childress claimed to have been inspired by the actress Georgia Burke, with whom she shared a Broadway stage in *Anna Lucasta*. "Georgia Burke was a person like Wiletta who went along, went along, went along," Childress said in an interview. "Some days she said, 'I'm tired of it.' And I thought, 'She has the spirit . . .'" Wiletta is a woman and an actor who goes along, goes along, goes along until, today, she doesn't, and that is the substance of the drama. But the question does nag the mind: What was the substance of all that "going along"?

This edition of *Trouble in Mind* actually suggests an answer to that question, restoring a final monologue for Wiletta that has never seen publication, in which she more or less catalogs the way in which the average Black-identified actor has been historically cornered into playing everything but a truthful version of a self—ceding the very stuff of her life, her very being in time, to an actual denial of it—and one does get the sense, from Childress, that the cost of this unceasing grind could be one's sanity. In order to keep hers, Wiletta must first wrap her head around her own understanding and thus begin with questioning the understanding of those in power.

"Talkin' 'bout the truth is anything I can believe," she says early in the play's climactic scene, once her passive-aggressive conflict with Manners has spilled over into actual aggression: "Well, I don't believe this." She has challenged a key plot turn in *Chaos*, during which she, the Black protagonist's mother, more or less wittingly hands her son over to a murderous white mob, somehow convinced it's the right thing to do. Why, Wiletta asks, do the director and the playwright believe any mother—let alone a Black one—would walk her child to the gallows, unless they did not believe that she was a human being? And, beneath that, sits another question: Why would this woman not be a human being? And, beneath that, another: Why do they expect Wiletta to be able to play anything other than a human being unless they didn't believe, on some level, that she wasn't one? And with this clapback, Childress cuts to the heart of one of the most enduring hypocrisies of the American theater and letters writ large: a perennial desire to present Black life onstage without a willingness to afford it the capacity for self-determination.

Trouble in Mind is set in the mid-twentieth century but what is perhaps most surprising about one's first encounter with this almost seventy-year-old play is just how elegant and present tense it feels in its preoccupation with the soulless commercial exploitation of Black suffering, the existential difficulty of "authentic" representation, the human right to self-definition, and the tyranny of white creative do-gooderism. In that way, it is a high point in the practice of institutional critique that seems to run like a vein through the corpus of American drama and, ironically enough, counts among its master practitioners an overwhelming number of Black voices. The play by a minority playwright deconstructing just what is wrong with the art she has been compelled to work with and within is almost a rite of passage. Countless contemporary examples abound, perhaps some of the most iconic in recent memory being *The Colored Museum* by George C. Wolfe, *Fairview* by Jackie Sibbles Drury, and *A Strange Loop* by Michael R. Jackson, the last two being back-to-back winners of the Pulitzer Prize. But credit must be given to *Trouble in Mind* as being among the first, the most elegant, and the most powerful.

There are countless theories as to why exactly this is, but the most convincing to me has to do with the American theater's undeniable roots in blackface minstrelsy. By the time Black artists—not to even think of Black audiences—were even allowed in the buildings, there was already a dark and deeply established practice for how the Sons of Ham might be convincingly depicted and appropriately received onstage. (It is worth noting that Childress's first marriage had been to Alvin Childress of *Amos 'n' Andy* fame and had not ended happily.) The theater, despite what it might want to tell itself, has never been as flexible or immediately responsive to the issues of its time in the way that other arts have proven to be. When it comes to social progress, it is often the last creative form to the party. This means that it is not a surprise that audiences today can still go to a play and encounter story tropes and depictions of Others of all stripes—racialized, gendered, etc.—that feel a generation old and unsavory.

. . .

Much—almost too much—has been made about Alice Childress's refusal to bring a compromised version of *Trouble in Mind* to Broadway and become the first play by an African-American woman to tread those boards. (Lorraine Hansberry's *A Raisin in the Sun* would seal that deal only a couple of years later.) In fact, at a recent celebrated revival of *Trouble in Mind*, this factoid was announced over speakers during the curtain speech, wedged between a plea to turn off one's cell phone and the beginning of the show proper. The result, for some, was a disappointing sense that the theater itself was somehow upstaging the play, almost as if it wanted to be congratulated for righting some wrong of history—or worse: that the play needed some sort of justification for its being presented. Meanwhile, this theater has historically had one of the worst track records for diversity on its programming and, concurrently on one of its other stages, another, even more contemporary revival, was running about a Black mother who bore an uneasy resemblance to the mother Wiletta was being demanded to figure out how to play in *Chaos*. The irony, once you caught it, was almost unbearable.

Fetishing the life of this play, which was long out of print until only recently due the inspired advocacy of longtime Childress collaborator and friend Kathy Perkins, over the play itself can obscure the fact that Childress actually did try to work very hard *with* the producers and systems of the time to create a commercially possible version of *Trouble in Mind*, but that ultimately both parties lost interest; that the final version of this play is not the same play that premiered Off-Broadway in 1955 but the product of decades and decades of thought and reworking. But, most importantly, making this play about the history that never was, obscures the piercing truthfulness of the observation and arguments that the play contains, observations and arguments *which still hold true* for the average Black-identified theater maker, actor, playwright, and director alike. It points to an essential issue still at the heart of this art form as we practice it. This play shouldn't be celebrated as merely a lost classic. It should be revered, feared, and studied with humility—if not shame—as a lost indictment.

> Trouble in mind, I'm blue
> My poor heart is beating slow
> Never had no trouble in my life before

That there is a deep relationship between the blues and just about every other form of African-American expression is a secret only to the unobservant and, in the theater, this long-running symbiosis meets perhaps its pinnacle in the oeuvre of August Wilson. In countless interviews, Wilson himself cited a chance encounter with a blues recording by Bessie Smith as the genesis of his own realization of self as an artist. "The universe stuttered," he is quoted as saying, "and everything fell into place." But in this urgency to locate the genesis of all Black American artistic genius in the soil of this truly unique and truly Black musical form, we can overlook the fact that it is often a Black and *female* voice which is the vehicle for this transformation. Black female genius is categorically overlooked again and again as the wellspring of momentous instances of wider cultural production.

In this spirit, it seems only appropriate that *Trouble in Mind* be the inaugural entry in Illuminations, a new series through TCG Books, edited by myself, that seeks to shine light on and bring new attention to under-recognized and, in some cases, truly undiscovered classics of the American drama. It was Childress herself, when confronted with the label of being "ahead of her time," who responded: "People aren't ahead of their time, they are choked during their time."

I hope that it is the work of this series to give these artists and their works the fresh and long overdue air to breathe again and live.

Brooklyn, New York
January 2022

BRANDEN JACOBS-JENKINS *is a Brooklyn-based writer and award-winning theater artist. His plays include* Girls, Gloria, Everybody, War, Appropriate, An Octoroon, *and* Neighbors. *He teaches at The University of Texas at Austin.*

ALICE CHILDRESS

Born in 1916 and raised during the Harlem Renaissance under the watchful eye of her beloved maternal grandmother, Alice Childress grew up to become first an actress and then a playwright and novelist. A founding member of the American Negro Theatre, she wrote her first play, *Florence*, in 1949. The script was written in one night on a dare from close friend and actor Sidney Poitier, who had told Childress that he did not think a great play could be written overnight. She proved him wrong, and the play was produced Off-Broadway in 1949.

Childress became the first African-American woman to have a play receive a professional production in New York City in 1952 with *Gold Through the Trees*. In 1955, Childress's play, *Trouble in Mind*, opened at the Greenwich Mews Theatre, Off-Broadway, to critical and popular success. The play immediately drew interest from producers for a Broadway transfer. In an ironic twist echoing the tribulations of the characters in the play itself, the producers wanted changes to the script to make it more palatable to a commercial audience. Childress refused to compromise her artistic vision, and the play never opened on Broadway, ending her chances of being the first African-American woman playwright to have a play on Broadway. *Trouble in Mind* received a well-reviewed Off-Broadway revival in 1998 by the Negro Ensemble Company and has since been produced by many regional theaters throughout the United States and at Theatre Royal Bath in England.

Childress was the first African-American woman to direct an Off-Broadway play with the production of *Wedding Band* at the New York Shakespeare Festival in 1972.

Childress is known for *A Hero Ain't Nothin' but a Sandwich*, her 1973 novel about a thirteen-year-old Black boy addicted to heroin, which was subsequently made into a movie in 1978. Plays written by Childress include *Just a Little Simple* (1950); *Wedding Band: A Love/Hate Story in Black and White* (1966); *Wine in the Wilderness* (1968); *String* (1969); *Mojo: A Black Love Story* (1970); *When the Rattlesnake Sounds*, a children's play (1976); *Let's Hear It for the Queen*, a children's play (1976); *Sea Island Song* (1977); and *Gullah* (1984). Her novels include *Like One of the Family: Conversations from a Domestic's Life* (1956); *A Short Walk* (1979), nominated for the Pulitzer Prize for Fiction; *Rainbow Jordan* (1981); and *Those Other People* (1989).

Childress died in New York in 1994. Throughout her career, she worked diligently to reveal the experiences of Black people in America, especially those of Black women. As Childress herself once said, "I concentrate on portraying the have-nots in a have society."

ILLUMINATIONS FROM TCG BOOKS is dedicated to revisiting plays known and loved, and paying tribute to works previously overlooked. To help restore the work of Black playwrights to its rightful place in the canon, the Illuminations series, curated and edited by Branden Jacobs-Jenkins, began by publishing classic plays by Black playwrights. The series was launched with the 2022 publication of Alice Childress's 1955 play *Trouble in Mind*, featuring an essay by Jacobs-Jenkins. Over its first five years, Illuminations will publish two works annually, each with an essay written by a noted playwright or theater maker. Mellon Foundation has been invaluable to this initiative.